WHOLE FOOD BABY

200 nutritionally balanced recipes for a healthy start

To E & P, you are the apples of my eye.

A Quantum Book

Copyright © 2016 Quantum Books Ltd

First edition for North America published in 2016 by
Barron's Educational Series, Inc.

All inquiries should be addressed to:
Barron's Educational Series, Inc.
250 Wireless Boulevard
Hauppauge, New York 11788
www.barronseduc.com

ISBN: 978-1-4380-0832-5

Library of Congress Control Number: 2016934104

QUMWFBB

This book was conceived, designed, and produced by:
Quantum Books Ltd
6 Blundell Street
London N7 9BH
United Kingdom

Printed in China by 1010 Printing International Ltd.

9 8 7 6 5 4 3 2 1

Disclaimer: The information in this book is for
informational purposes only and should not be relied
upon as recommending or promoting any specific diet or
practice. It is not intended as a guide to how to feed your
child or to replace the advice of a nutritionist, physician,
or medical practitioner. Knowledge of nutrition and
childcare is constantly evolving and you are encouraged
to consult other sources and make independent
judgments about the issues discussed in this book.
Neither the publisher nor the author is engaged in
rendering nutritional, medical, or other professional
advice or services.

There is the possibility of allergic or other adverse
reactions from the use of any ingredients mentioned
in this book. You should seek the advice of your doctor
or other qualified health provider with any questions
you may have, especially in relation to infants with
medical conditions or allergies. You should not use the
information in this book as a substitute for medication
or other treatment prescribed by your medical
practitioner.

The authors, editors, and publisher make no
representations or warranties with respect to the
accuracy, completeness, fitness for a particular purpose
or currency of the contents of this book and exclude all
liability to the extent permitted by law for any errors or
omissions and for any loss damage or expense (whether
direct or indirect) suffered by anyone relying on any
information contained in this book.

Michele Olivier

Nutritional Evaluators: Leslie L. Barton M.D. and Anne Marie Berggren

WHOLE FOOD BABY

200 nutritionally balanced recipes for a healthy start

BARRON'S

CHAPTER ONE
Introducing Whole Foods

CHAPTER TWO
First Foods

CHAPTER THREE
Next Steps

CHAPTER FOUR
First Finger Foods

CHAPTER FIVE
Moving On + Four Years

CHAPTER SIX
Nutritional Information

CONTENTS

Note

Chapters Two to Four are intended as recipes to use in conjunction with breastfeeding or formula. Chapter Five includes recipes for growing children that are best suited for children over the age of four.

INTRODUCTION

Hey you, come on over and pull up a chair. I just made a cup of coffee, and we have a lot to catch up on. Let's start with me, I'm bossy like that.

My baby food–making story starts like any other mompreneur story—it features a frustrated mom, a ridiculous problem, and an easy solution. Six months after my eldest daughter, Ellie, was born, I opened a container of store-bought baby food, took one bite, and then swore my precious baby girl would never eat such bland and boring food. It was time for me to get to work and make my own!

At the time I was slightly overwhelmed with the thought of making my own baby purees. So I packed up my blender and headed over to my parent's house, where my mom and I made over 800 ounces of baby purees in one afternoon. For that amount of puree, team work definitely makes the dream work... but overall I was amazed at how simple the process really was. Turns out baby Ellie liked the purees even more than I did, and before long all of my puree back-stock was gone... all 800 ounces! Ellie just loved (and still loves) delicious purees that are full of mouth-watering flavors and fun spices and herbs.

Three years later, I have quit my day job to pursue my passion of making healthy but delicious recipes that babies, toddlers, and kids will actually eat and enjoy. These days you will find me in my yoga pants, while taste testing; photographing; and writing about purees, muffins, nut butters, and family-friendly recipes. I have taken my dream and turned it into a career.

All of the recipes in this book are easy to make (because every mom I know is beyond busy); taste amazing; and are full of nutrient-dense foods that will help your baby grow strong and healthy. Whole foods will provide the array of micronutrients that your baby needs to thrive to their full potential, just as nature intended. Healthy fats will support optimal brain development and assist the absorption of fat-soluble vitamins. Meats and fish will provide crucial protein, iron, and zinc. Complex carbohydrates will provide energy along with B vitamins. And a rainbow of colored plant foods provide vitamins and minerals to optimize growth and development.

Using whole foods may sound intimidating, but they are really easy to cook and the healthiest form of food. You are looking to make baby food from the source; nothing processed or packaged; food that is straight from the vine, ground, tree,

or bush. Whole foods are not only the healthiest food source for your baby, but they are also cheaper than packaged forms of food. Saving money while eating healthy—that's a win-win in my view.

But let's get back to the taste, because it doesn't matter how healthy the puree is if your baby doesn't eat it. Purees such as Peach, Plum, and Blueberry Puree (see page 42); Thai Chicken and Green Bean Puree (see page 51); and Pear, Strawberry, and Flaxseed Puree (see page 36) have been taste tested by not only my own wee ones but also by my friend's babies and friends of friend's babies whom I don't even know. I am like a baby food mule, delivering healthy baby food to all areas in Denver!

Now it's your turn. How are you feeling? Tired? Stressed? Emotional? Totally normal as a new parent, and unfortunately it only gets a little better with time. Hungry? That we can work on. If you answered "yes" to all of the above, it sounds like you have found the right place to be—where all foodies, parents, and kids belong. How about another cup of coffee before we get started? I want to hear all about what amazing things your little one is doing these days.

xo, Michele

Safety First

This is not a book about how to feed your baby or what or when they should eat—it is a recipe book to be used alongside the guidance provided to you by your pediatrician. The recipes and advice given by the author are drawn from her experiences as a mom and baby food blogger. Do check with your pediatrician if you are considering moving on from breastmilk.

GETTING STARTED

The recipes in this book have been designed with the busy mom in mind—each is quick and easy to prepare, with tips on how to make a batch in advance and store for use later. Most importantly, these recipes have been created to provide your baby with all the essential nutrients they need for growth and development. Use the nutritional key (see page 9) to quickly guide you.

How to Find the Recipe You Need

The recipes are divided into chapters by eating stage: for basic purees to excite your baby's taste buds, turn to First Foods; to introduce more texture to your little one's purees, try Next Steps; First Finger Foods is packed with fun ideas to encourage your baby to start feeding themselves; and for snacks and meals for older toddlers, the Moving On chapter has you covered. You can also use the indexes at the back of the book to find recipes by key nutrient or nutritional benefit.

Essential Information

Before you start, find out the yield and serving size for each recipe, plus the preparation and cooking times and storage information.

Tips and Tricks

The *Also Good With* suggestions give even more ideas for adding a delicious twist to your baby's meal or sneaking in an extra nutritional boost. For an in-depth look at specific ingredients and nutrition for baby, check out the *Closer Look* panels.

Whole Food Baby Nutritional Key

Each recipe has been tagged with key nutritional benefits for your baby (see page 9), so you can choose the right recipe for your little one's needs.

NOTES FOR THE RECIPES IN THIS BOOK

CHOOSING A RECIPE FOR YOUR BABY

Broth

Dairy and Non-Dairy Milks

Honey for Babies

Nuts and Seeds

Cooking With Fish

Organic Produce

Combination Purees

Reheating Food

Finding the Right Recipe

Nutritional Guidelines

Nutrition for Baby

Turn to pages 164–173 at the back of the book to find additional nutritional information, including useful notes on the recipes in this book. There are also comprehensive indexes for each of the *Whole Food Baby* keys (see below), along with the top five recipes for vital nutrients to support growth and development, such as iron and protein.

Explaining the *Whole Food Baby* Nutritional Key

Every recipe is tagged to help you understand the nutritional benefits different foods can help provide for your baby. Simply flick through the pages to find foods that will provide vital protein for growing babies, give an extra dose of iron, or help support brain development.

 Bone Growth—Healthy bones are the foundation of your baby's growth. These foods are high in calcium, vitamin C, vitamin K, and potassium.

 Brain Boost—Rich in omega-3 fatty acids, choline, and other essential nutrients your baby needs for a healthy, functioning brain.

 Iron Rich—Crucial for growth and development, iron helps prevent fatigue and weakness in baby.

 Vitamin Rich—Essential for a healthy immune system, vitamin-rich foods also help to support growth.

 Protein Rich—These foods will help ensure your baby is getting enough protein for healthy skin, hair, bones, and muscle.

 Good Source of Fiber—To help combat constipation in babies, these foods are high in the soluble and insoluble fiber that the digestive tract needs.

 Bright Eyes—Foods rich in lutein and vitamin A help to support healthy vision.

 High in Omega-3—Omega-3 fats, DHA, and ALA are all essential for eye and brain health, and for boosting the immune system.

 Eases Digestion—Helps soothe the digestive tract and tummy when introducing new foods.

 Immunity Builder—Rich in vitamins C and A, as well as zinc to help support the immune system.

 Antioxidant—A diet rich in antioxidants and phytonutrients helps protect cells from damage. These foods are rich in vitamins C and E, omega-3s, and zinc.

 Superfood—Natural, whole foods that are high in nutrients and antioxidants that are essential for growing babies and toddlers.

 Source of Complex Carbs—These foods will help to provide the complex carbs that the brain needs for energy.

 Super Puree—Combining multiple superfoods, these meals are rich in antioxidants and nutrients.

 Baby-Led Weaning—These recipes are perfect for when your baby starts wanting to feed themselves.

WHY MAKE YOUR OWN BABY FOOD?

While it does take a little time to cook, puree, and freeze homemade baby food, at the end of the day, making your own baby food provides more nutritious meals for your baby and allows you complete control over what ingredients you use and what flavors you serve. A win-win in my opinion!

1 Planning Ahead

To save time, I have always found it easiest to make a bunch of different purees on one weekend a month, giving me a big freezer assortment to use for the weeks ahead. Other moms love to make little batches throughout the week whenever they can fit it in. A fun option is to have a baby food–making party—invite some other new mommies over to your house and get to work. Whichever method you use, freezing the purees is key to making the process easier, so invest in a few ice cube or puree trays.

2 Taste

Roasting, steaming, and sautéing your baby's food all contribute to the overall taste of the puree, and when you make your own baby food, you get to control this cooking method and how the flavors will develop. I dare you to try the Banana and Clove Puree (page 37) and tell me that you can get that in a jar. It isn't going to happen. All of these recipes are designed to highlight the produces' natural taste and bring out foods' amazing qualities.

3 Ingredients

When making your own baby food, you get to be in control over the produce and ingredients that go into your baby's meals. Being able to pick out colorful, ripe, organic, and seasonal ingredients for your baby to enjoy at the height of freshness is a great way to teach them how to eat with the cycles of the crops. Bonus—it's also cheaper to buy what is in season!

Watch Out for Salt

One of the many advantages of making your own baby food is knowing exactly what ingredients are going into it. How much salt is in your baby's or toddler's meals is particularly important to keep an eye on.

Salty foods are not recommended for babies, as salt will stress a baby's kidneys and a high level of salt could be too much for them to process. By making your own baby food, you will be able to monitor the sodium levels in your baby's food, and by feeding them fresh, whole foods, salt levels will be naturally low.

Toddlers, on the other hand, do need a small amount of salt in their diets. The problem is that toddlers in the United States are currently consuming on average three times the recommended amount of salt. Almost all of this surplus of salt is from processed foods such as crackers, breads, cereals, chips, dry soup mixes, and frozen meals. This doesn't mean that all salt is bad. Unrefined sea salt and Himalayan salt (pink salt) contain a number of minerals such as magnesium, calcium, iodine, and potassium which can help with metabolism, hydration, hormone production, the immune system, and are essential for the development of the brain. So when making homemade food calling for salt, opt for the unrefined variety. Unrefined sea salt and Himalayan salt can both be found in most grocery stores. When purchasing packaged foods for your baby or toddler, choose low-sodium and organic brands whenever possible.

4 Nutrition

A cooked apple is a cooked apple, as some believe. That would be true, except the fruits and vegetables used in packaged baby food are heated to extremely high temperatures for long periods of time in order for the jars to be shelf stable for a year or more! This results in food that has lost the vast majority of the nutrients it contained. Sadly, the jars of baby food on the shelf are most likely older than your baby. On the other hand, the produce you use to make homemade baby food is heated at lower temperatures and for the shortest amount of time possible, resulting in more nutrient-dense baby food. Cooking produce for a shorter amount of time also means you are in and out of the kitchen faster—score!

5 Pride

This one is a personal reward, but I always have a sense of pride after I make a big batch of healthy purees for my babies (cue happy dance). Taking the extra time, when we all know there isn't much of it, to make healthy food for your baby is something that you should be proud of. By taking the time and making your baby's eating a priority, you are not only giving their bodies a healthy head start, but you are also setting them up for developing a lifelong healthy relationship with healthy food.

WHEN IS YOUR BABY READY FOR FOODS?

Deciding when your baby is ready to start purees and complementary foods alongside breastfeeding or formula can be difficult. There is a wealth of information available from websites, books, and wellness organizations, which can be a bit overwhelming. The key is to remember that each baby is different and to do what feels right for you.

What the Experts Say

There are a number of great resources that provide guidelines on feeding your baby, including national health guidelines and organizations such as the American Academy of Pediatrics, the World Health Organization, and UNICEF. You can also always talk to your pediatrician about your baby's individual needs.

Most leading organizations recommend that babies are exclusively breastfed, or fed with formula milk, until six months, when purees and complementary foods can start being introduced alongside breastmilk or formula milk. The World Health Organization, UNICEF, and American Family Physician all recommend continuing breastfeeding or formula milk alongside other foods until at least one year of age, with optimal health benefits if breastfeeding is continued until two years of age. Breastfeeding is a great way to give your baby all the nutrients that they need in their first months and has many health benefits for both mommy and baby. (For more information on recommended feeding and nutrient guidelines, see pages 164–173.)

It is also important to give your baby the best possible introduction to all the amazing, healthy foods out there. And that is what this book is about: starting your baby out on their culinary adventure. The first experiences of food, taste, flavor, and texture are pivotal in the development of our relationship with food and can shape eating habits into adulthood. Let me reassure you: picky eating is not genetic or unavoidable, food habits can be changed, and the best time to shape these is in childhood. Recent studies have found that children need to be introduced to new flavors in small amounts as many as 15 or 20 times before

they accept them. So don't despair when your baby spits out their beet puree for the fourth time!

In my experience, all babies are different and have different approaches to food and feeding. Some children may be eager to start trying food out before six months old, whereas others might remain uninterested for a little longer.

How to Read the Signs That Your Baby Is Ready to Start Foods

There isn't a certain start date that tells you when your baby is ready to begin their culinary adventure. Generally, babies are ready around six months of age. The best way to tell if your baby is ready is to listen to their silent cues.

- Can your baby sit all by themselves?
- Is your baby holding their head and neck in an upright position?
- Does your baby reach for, or eye, the food that you are eating?
- Is your baby hungry more often and not satisfied by their normal amount of breastmilk or formula?
- Has their weight doubled since birth?

When you can answer "yes" to most of the above cues, then your baby is ready to start eating. If they aren't quite there yet, no worries; you can spend that time whipping up and freezing more batches of delicious baby purees for when they are ready.

If you decide that your baby is ready to start weaning before six months, avoid foods containing gluten, eggs, shellfish, nuts, seeds, and soft and unpasteurized cheeses, and ask your pediatrician for advice.

How the Recommended Sequence of Introducing Complementary Foods Corresponds with Food Textures and Feeding Styles

AGE OF INFANT BY MONTH	BIRTH	1	2	3	4	5	6	7	8	9	10	11	12
AGE GROUPING	BIRTH–3 MONTHS				4 MONTHS–6MONTHS			6 MONTHS–8 MONTHS		8 MONTHS–12 MONTHS			
SEQUENCE OF INTRODUCING FOODS	BREASTMILK OR INFANT FORMULA				** Complementary foods								
TEXTURE OF COMPLEMENTARY FOODS					Strained/pureed (thin consistency for cereal)								
									Mashed				
											Ground/finely chopped		
												Chopped	
FEEDING STYLE	Breastfeeding/bottle feeding												
					Spoon feeding								
					Cup feeding								
											Self feeding/ feeding finger foods		

Special Notes for Chart:

The green highlighted section in the chart above represents the age range when most infants are ready to begin consuming complementary foods. The American Academy of Pediatrics (AAP) Section on Breastfeeding recommends exclusive breastfeeding for the first six months of life. The AAP Committee on Nutrition recommends that, in developed countries, complementary foods may be introduced between four and six months of age. This is a population-based recommendation, and the timing of introduction of complementary foods for an individual infant may differ.

Breastmilk is the top recommended food for babies under one year—the recipes in this book are not intended to replace it. Breastfeeding or formula should be continued alongside other foods until at least one year of age.

** Complementary foods include vegetables, fruits, meat, and other protein-rich foods modified to an appropriate texture (strained, pureed, chopped, etc.) for the infant's developmental readiness.

HOW TO START WEANING

Your baby is showing all the signs that they are ready to eat. Hooray! Now what? For many parents, this first feeding can be extremely stressful. Relax, have fun, and get your camera ready; this stage is a fun (and messy) one.

Step-by-Step Baby Weaning

Weaning is when you gradually start to introduce your baby to a range of foods, alongside breastmilk or formula, until they are eating the same foods as the rest of the family. There is no foolproof guide to baby's first feeding, but here are some top tips to help you and your baby:

1 Start by having your baby's first meal at a time of day when your baby is happy and slightly full (a meal right before nap time isn't going to be a good time for anyone involved).

2 Gently heat a small portion (1 ounce) of puree, and either spoon feed this portion or place a couple of dollops of puree on your baby's tray and let them play and feed themselves.

3 Have fun and encourage your baby to eat the puree in a reassuring manner.

4 Chances are your baby is either going to eat the puree right up or throw the spoon at you. Both are great options (although the spoon throwing does get messy).

5 Since at this point all of babies' daily calories are coming from breastmilk or formula, feeding them purees is for the pure experience of eating.

6 If at any point your baby closes their mouth and starts turning their head away from the food, it's time to stop the meal for the day. Don't be discouraged; it takes some time for a baby to learn this new milestone. Be patient and try again the next day.

Baby Weaning Top Tips

Never leave your baby alone while eating.

Make sure your baby is sitting up straight and facing forward—using a high chair is best. This will allow your baby to explore foods better and will mean they are less likely to choke.

Patience is key: Don't try to rush the meal or force your baby to eat more. Go at the pace of your little one.

A Baby's Eating Stages

Instead of putting exact timelines and month ranges of when your baby should be eating what food, which I find intimidating, I like to think of these as feeding stages: starting, combinations, chunky, and finger foods. Each baby is going to explore these stages at their own rate. It's important to not get caught up in what age your baby is eating what. The important thing to focus on is providing a variety of healthy foods and making sure that your baby is increasing the amount they eat every week.

STARTING OUT • This stage starts roughly around 4–6 months and includes simple (yet yummy) purees, such as Apple and Clove Puree (page 32), Green Bean and Cilantro Puree (page 50), and Carrot and Cumin Puree (page 48).

COMBINATION PUREES • As long as there aren't any allergies in the immediate family (parents, siblings), combination purees can start shortly after your baby has tried a handful of simple purees. New foods should always be introduced as simple purees first, before including them in combination purees for your baby.

CHUNKY PUREES • Once your baby has mastered combination purees and is eating a good amount of purees at several meals a day, you can start to introduce chunky purees. These can be made by simply not pureeing combination purees all the way, or by adding in whole grains or chunks of meat or fish.

FINGER FOODS • Finger foods can be started at any time of weaning—at the very beginning, during the purees stage, or after the chunky puree stage. I personally like to offer a couple of small finger foods while I am spoon feeding purees. This gives your baby a chance to work on their pincer grasp while getting a good amount of purees into their bellies. Be sure to cut up any finger foods into very small pieces to avoid any choking hazards.

BABY'S EXPLORATION OF FOOD THROUGH TASTE AND TEXTURE

Every time your baby tries a new puree, it is a brand new experience for them! Love it, hate it, or somewhere in between, they are going to have a reaction to every food you make and serve. So enjoy introducing them to all the delicious new tastes, flavors, and textures of whole foods.

Introducing New Tastes

Have fun with introducing your baby to different tastes. Get ready to watch in amazement as they love some purees and grab the spoon out of your hand to get more in their mouths, and don't get too disappointed on the other days when their mouths stay sealed shut. While it is extremely easy to get frustrated when your baby doesn't like a puree you have made, don't give up. It can take up to 15 tries for a baby to decide if they actually like a puree or not. It took me 13 tries, seven different combinations, and five different spices to get baby Parker to enjoy the taste of acorn squash! You can also be reassured that your baby will be getting most of their calorie and nutrient requirements from breastmilk and formula for some time; at this stage, it is all about introducing your little one to delicious new flavors from whole foods.

They say that variety is the spice of life, so don't be afraid to give your baby new flavors to try out. Providing a range of healthy and colorful foods means that you are also providing a range of nutrients that your baby needs for healthy growth and development. It is also a great way to introduce your baby to all the flavors and tastes out there. The recipes in this book include everything from sweet, fruity favorites—such as apple and pear—to vegetables including broccoli, beets, and bell pepper.

Introducing New Textures

Once your baby has gotten the hang of eating all of their mouth-watering combinations with simple spices, it is time to introduce them to the world of texture. Just as feeding them sweet potatoes for the first time is a new taste experience for them, it is the same when introducing purees with slight chunks. Experiment with different textures, such as grains, meat, and fish, or less finely pureed produce, and see how your baby does with this new world of chunky food. I also like to start to introduce (if you haven't already) soft finger foods at this point. Having a few chopped blueberries, avocado chunks, or pieces of white fish to try while you feed them purees is a great way to encourage your baby to work their little hands and fill up on healthy purees at the same time.

solid foods

Best Starter Foods for Your Baby

My only rule for what and when to introduce a food to your baby is this—if it is a whole food, then you can go crazy, have fun, and let your baby explore this amazing world of food. Exceptions are honey, citrus, and undercooked eggs, which should be avoided until one year of age. Infants and young children should not eat any whole nuts or seeds, whole grapes, or large chunks or fruit or vegetables as these may be choking hazards. Chop fruit and veggies into pea size pieces or puree for your little one to enjoy. For the most nutrient-dense produce, look for ripe, colorful fruit and vegetables that are in season, local, and organic.

- **Fruit:** Apples, pears, mangoes, avocado, bananas, peaches, blueberries
- **Vegetables:** Sweet potatoes, carrots, asparagus, peas, butternut squash, zucchini, red bell peppers
- **Dairy:** Egg yolks, plain whole-milk yogurt
- **Meat:** Beef, chicken, fish, lamb
- **Grains:** Quinoa, millet, oats, lentils
- **Spices and herbs:** Cinnamon, cumin, cloves, nutmeg, cilantro, basil, parsley, thyme

Chunky puree

Puree

hard-boiled eggs

peas

olives

My Favorite Simple Finger Foods

These easy finger foods don't need extended instructions; they are simple enough for anyone to toss together in a couple of minutes. Dense in nutrients and full of flavor, these soft finger foods are perfect for babies over six months of age. For younger babies, cut up finger foods into small, pea-size pieces to make sure there is no choking hazard. Older toddlers can try whole blueberries and raspberries, but slice these smaller if in any doubt.

- Blueberries with a splash of orange juice
- Peach chunks drizzled sparingly with vanilla extract
- Olives, pitted and sliced
- Avocado chunks with lime juice
- Steamed peas tossed in coconut oil
- Raspberries
- Chopped hard-boiled eggs with Himalayan sea salt (only add salt for older toddlers)
- Mangoes with mint
- Roasted corn with chili powder
- Feta, cut into cubes (for older toddlers, as salty)
- Pasteurized blue cheese, cut into cubes (for older toddlers)

mango

avocado

raspberries

peach

blueberries

Safety First: Avoid Choking

To minimize any risk of choking, avoid hard vegetables or fruits such as carrots and apple pieces. Gently cooking foods such as carrots and apples is an ideal way to prepare delicious finger foods for your baby, as it makes them softer and easier to chew. Small, round foods such as grapes, cherry tomatoes, and whole blueberries should be avoided for young babies. If you are serving these foods to your little one, make sure that you cut them up into very small pieces. Be careful with foods such as sausages that have skin, or fish with bones, making sure that any skin or bones are removed before feeding. Always follow the guidelines for feeding babies and small children that are provided by your pediatrician.

SAMPLE MEAL PLANS

Having difficulty deciding which delicious recipe to prepare for your baby first? Here are a few sample daily menu plans for each of your baby's eating stages to get you started.

Just Starting Out*

Morning: Apple and Clove Puree (page 32)

Lunch: Butternut Squash and Olive Oil Puree (page 46)

Dinner: Asparagus and Mint Puree (page 53)

Little Chompers*

Morning: Peach, Plum, and Blueberry Puree (page 42)

Lunch: Beet and Mint Puree (page 56)

Snack: Avocado, Pineapple, and Banana Puree (page 38)

Dinner: Chicken, Pea, Broccoli, and Chive Puree (page 70)

* These meals should be in addition to your baby's normal amount of breastmilk or formula. Breastmilk and formula will continue to provide the bulk of your baby's nutritional and calorie needs for the first stages of weaning. It is recommended to continue breastfeeding until two years of age for optimal health benefits.

Big Chompers*

Morning: Millet, Coconut Milk, and Cinnamon Puree (page 64)

Lunch: Broccoli, Pear, Pea, and Mint Puree (page 49)

Snack: Banana, Apricot, Peach, and Chia Seed Puree (page 37)

Dinner: Salmon, Carrot, Lemon, and Shallot Puree (page 74)

Finger Food Meal*

Morning: Simmered Apples, Cloves, and Ginger and Chopped Hard-boiled Eggs with Himalayan Salt (pages 80 and 20)

Lunch: Roasted Sweet Potatoes and Paprika and Roasted Beets and Thyme (pages 84 and 86)

Snack: Blueberries with a Splash of Orange Juice (page 20)

Dinner: Salmon, Lime, and Parsley and Avocado Chunks with Lime Juice (pages 89 and 20)

Toddler Meal

Morning: Leek, Zucchini, and Thyme Mini Quiches; Creamy Cinnamon and Vanilla Fruit Dip (pages 144 and 126)

Lunch: Turkey, Cucumber, Gouda, and Blackberry Sandwich Station and Cinnamon Sweet Potato Crunchers (pages 147 and 138)

Snack: Toasted Coconut and Dark Chocolate Balls of Energy (page 134)

Dinner: Sun-dried Tomato and Basil Meatballs; Farro with Basil and Olive Oil; and Steamed Green Beans with Lemon Zest (pages 150, 90, and 86)

SETTING UP YOUR KITCHEN

To make feeding your baby delicious whole foods even easier, make sure you have a well-stocked kitchen with all the essential ingredients and equipment ready to grab and go when you get that precious hour to yourself.

Equipment

Chances are that you already have all of the kitchen equipment you need to make homemade baby purees. While the all-in-one baby food steamers and blenders are nice timesavers, I find that the standard equipment I already own provides a broader variety of tastes, textures, and flavors. Useful things to have on hand include:

- Baking sheet
- Steamer basket
- Medium and large saucepan
- Sharp knife
- Cutting board
- Spatula
- Vegetable peeler
- Blender or food processor
- Ice cube trays, puree trays, or portion-sized freezer jars to freeze purees in
- Reusable pouches for easy on-the-go meals
- Glass or BPA-free containers for purees
- Weaning spoons, sipper cups, and baby bowls and plates for serving

Best for Babies

When it comes to produce for your baby, think fresh, in season, and colorful. These items are must-haves for making quick purees for your baby.

- Apples
- Bananas
- Berries
- Avocado
- Sweet potatoes
- Butternut squash
- Green beans
- Pears
- Broccoli
- Beets

Storing Foods and Freezing

Making up a whole batch of purees and popping them in the freezer is my preferred method of preparing meals for my girls. Simply freeze straight after preparation in meal-sized portions. You can purchase puree freezing trays; otherwise, ice cube trays and plastic sandwich bags also work well. To reheat, either microwave until heated all the way through, then cool; place in a small serving dish and thaw in the fridge overnight; or gently warm in a small skillet until heated all the way through, then cool. Always test the internal temperature of any reheated food before serving.

Food for Toddlers

Now that your toddler is eating a wider variety of foods, it's important to stock up on a range of ingredients so you can always have a quick snack on hand for your hungry little kiddo. I like to always have a variety of grains, nuts, and dried fruit stored in big Mason jars in my pantry.

DRIED FRUIT • Dried fruit can be incorporated into so many recipes—tossed in oatmeal, muffins, or energy balls, or used for a quick on-the-go snack.

- Raisins
- Blueberries
- Pineapple
- Apricot
- Golden raisins
- Apples
- Cranberries
- Dates

FROZEN FRUIT AND VEGETABLES • Picked at the peak of freshness and flash frozen, frozen fruit or vegetables are great to have when certain produce isn't in season. I also find that organic frozen produce is much more reasonably priced than fresh and a great way to afford organic produce on a tight budget.

- Strawberries
- Pineapple
- Green beans
- Broccoli
- Spinach
- Kale
- Mango
- Peaches
- Blueberries

NUTS AND SEEDS • Served as a quick snack or made into a tasty butter, nuts are a great protein-full item to keep stocked up on. Whole nuts and seeds are only suitable for children over four years of age (see page 115).

+4 years

- Almonds
- Cashews
- Sunflower seeds
- Pistachios
- Pumpkin seeds

WHOLE FOODS FOR BABIES AND TODDLERS

A fresh, ripe peach straight off the tree; carrots that still have dirt on them; basil that perfumes your entire kitchen—these fresh, whole foods are what nature has provided for your baby. They contain everything your little one needs in order to thrive in the early years of life, but they also teach your baby what to crave when they grow up.

Starting your baby off on colorful, fragrant, and delicious purees and finger foods will help refine your baby's budding palate and tempt their taste buds—until they reach two years of age (the picky stage), and then all bets are off the table.

Vegetables

These colorful vegetables are full of fiber, essential vitamins, and calcium that will help your baby grow; keep them full of energy; and help develop their bones, eyes, and internal organs. Also, by providing your baby with nutrient-rich vegetables, you will develop their palate into one that craves the taste of each vegetable and will help ease toddlers' picky phase.

- Carrots
- Sweet potatoes
- Green beans
- Asparagus
- Butternut squash
- Pumpkin
- Red bell peppers
- Broccoli
- Beets
- Spinach
- Kale

Fruit

Sweet, delicious fruit is a great source of antioxidants, essential vitamins, and fiber. As a healthy puree, finger food, snack, and even dessert, your baby's diet should be full of fruit. I like to serve fresh and seasonal fruit to my kiddos, but when something isn't in season, I buy the item in organic and frozen form, and it works equally well in almost all recipes.

- Apples
- Mangoes
- Pears
- Peaches
- Blueberries
- Strawberries
- Bananas
- Avocado

Whole Grains

Whole grains (grains found in their natural state) are full of fiber, protein, and calcium, and some even have all of the B vitamins. Grains are not only a great way to make babies and toddlers feel satisfied and full, but they also help them have enough energy to play throughout the day. Pureed until smooth, mixed into a chunky puree, or served as a finger food, it's easy to find delicious ways to use whole grains in your baby's food.

- Quinoa
- Oats
- Millet
- Barley
- Brown rice
- Buckwheat

Meat and Fish

Meat is full of protein, folate, and iron, so introducing meat at an early age is a great way to replenish your baby's essential iron reserves. Fish is full of protein and omega-3 fatty acids that aid in brain, nerve, and eye development. While some babies will eat a simple puree of meat or fish, I find mixing them into tasty combinations is the best way to encourage your baby to enjoy their bold flavors. Remember, it is always best to introduce new foods to your baby in a simple puree first.

- Beef
- Chicken
- Pork
- Turkey
- White fish (tilapia, grouper, sole)
- Wild salmon

Dairy

Dairy foods, which includes yogurt and cheese, are a key source of protein, fat, and calcium for children over the age of one. Because growing kids need 30–40 percent of their calories from a healthy fat source, I would purchase these ingredients in whole-fat, organic, and pasture-raised quality. If you want to wait before introducing animal milk to your toddler, use canned coconut milk or almond milk and avoid serving soy milk or soy products, as they are heavily processed. Plant-based milks are not equivalent to dairy milks as they lack the protein of dairy milks.

- Whole milk
- Whole-fat yogurt
- Cheese (feta, goats', cheddar, Gouda)
- Full-fat canned coconut milk
- Unsweetened almond milk

ADDING SPICES AND HERBS TO MEALS

Your baby's got taste! And this taste started before you were even aware of it—I'm talking about food taste here; we all know your baby is the cutest baby ever! Delicious spices will not only delight your baby's taste buds, but will also sneak in all kinds of great nutrients.

Early Taste Development

Remember when you were pregnant and eating that fresh spinach and strawberry salad with chives and crushed pepper? Or when you roasted sweet potatoes with thyme and paprika, or even when you took the day off from eating well and had that ice cream with peaches and cloves? Your baby was already enjoying all of those yummy tastes. Yes, that ice cream was giving your baby a culinary experience. Babies, just like adults, enjoy food that tastes and smells wonderful. They want to explore the world around them in as many ways as possible, and adding a pinch of cinnamon to apples, a dash of nutmeg to roasted carrots, or even a chopped sprig of mint to avocado will help them explore the world through their ever-growing palate.

Flavor and Nutrition

Not only do spices and herbs enhance the taste of your baby's food, they also have amazing medicinal properties. Cinnamon helps to boost brain power, mint can clear up congestion, ginger aids in digestion, and cloves boost the immune system. All of that with just a pinch of spice!

Top Spices and Herbs

Add some extra flavor and nutrients to your baby's meals with just a sprinkling of these:

Basil

Chives

Cilantro

Cinnamon

Cloves

Coriander

Cumin

Mild Curry

Mint

Nutmeg

Paprika

Thyme

Vanilla

dried mixed herbs

coriander

vanilla

paprika

cumin

cinnamon

nutmeg

cilantro

thyme

basil

APPLE AND CLOVE PUREE, PAGE 32

FIRST FOODS

This is it—your baby's first bite of food—so let's make it a good one! A bite full of smooth and creamy deliciousness will woo their taste buds and develop their little palate so they are ready to crave whole, colorful, and nutritious foods that will lead to a lifetime of healthy eating. Hopefully a couple less spoonfuls will be tossed in your direction if they are enjoying their food, too!

APPLE PUREES

Prep Time 5 minutes
Cook Time 15–25 minutes
Yield about 20–30 oz (560–850 g)
Storage 3 days in fridge or 2 months in freezer

Apples make a smooth and tasty starter puree, and you can also add apple to just about any other puree for a great combination. These fruits are loaded with two different types of fiber, vitamins A and E, folate, and potassium.

 ### APPLE AND CLOVE PUREE *(shown on page 30)*

This recipe is so good that it is embedded into my brain! It is a great starter puree or chunky applesauce for toddlers.

Ingredients:
- 5 eating apples, cored, peeled, and chopped (Fuji, Macintosh, Pink Lady)
- ¼ teaspoon ground cloves
- ½ cup (120 ml) water

Put the apples, cloves, and water in a medium saucepan. Cover and cook over medium heat for 15 minutes, stirring occasionally, or until apples are tender. Let cool slightly. Transfer all ingredients to a blender or food processor, and puree until smooth.

 ### variation | APPLE, PEACH, AND VANILLA PUREE

Make the basic apple puree using the main recipe (above), but omit the cloves and add 3 ripe pitted and peeled peaches. Increase the water to ¾ cup (180 ml). Heat for 15 minutes, stirring occasionally, or until the apples and peaches are both tender. Meanwhile, deseed ½ fresh vanilla bean by cutting the pod lengthwise and scraping out the seeds with the back of a knife (you can also use 2 teaspoons of high-quality vanilla bean extract). Transfer the apples, peaches, and vanilla seeds to a blender or food processor, and puree until smooth, adding additional water in ¼ cup (60 ml) increments if needed.

 ### variation | APPLE, BLACKBERRY, AND KALE PUREE

Make the basic apple puree using the main recipe (above), but omit the cloves and add 1 cup (140 g) blackberries (fresh or frozen) and ½ cup (35 g) packed, chopped, and destemmed kale. Heat for 15–20 minutes, stirring occasionally. Puree as instructed in the main recipe (above), adding additional water in ¼ cup (60 ml) increments if needed.

Also Good With: 1 teaspoon ground cinnamon or ½ teaspoon freshly grated ginger added in during the cooking time.

variation | CHICKEN, CARROT, APPLE, AND CUMIN PUREE

Make the basic apple puree using the main recipe (page 32), but omit the cloves and add 1 cubed boneless chicken breast, 4 peeled and chopped carrots, and 1 teaspoon ground cumin. Pour in enough low-sodium chicken broth or water to submerge all the ingredients, roughly 2 cups (480 ml). Bring to a boil, then reduce heat to low and simmer for 15 minutes or until the chicken is completely done. Let cool slightly. Use a slotted spoon to transfer all the ingredients to a blender or food processor, reserving the water in the saucepan. Puree until smooth, adding reserved water in ¼ cup (60 ml) increments if needed.

variation | SALMON, APPLE, SAGE, AND QUINOA PUREE

Start by bringing 3 cored, peeled, and chopped eating apples and 4 cups (960 ml) low- or no-sodium fish or vegetable broth or water to a boil in a large saucepan over high heat. Reduce heat to low and simmer. Add two 6 oz (175 g) salmon fillets, covering with additional broth if needed. Cook for 8–10 minutes or until the salmon is fully cooked. Break the cooked salmon into chunks, and use a slotted spoon to transfer the apples and salmon to a blender or food processor. Add 3 chopped sage leaves and puree until smooth, adding broth in ¼ cup (60 ml) increments if needed. Gently stir in 1 cup (180 g) cooked quinoa for a chunky puree or add quinoa to the blender and puree for a smoother consistency.

> **Combination Purees:**
> Always introduce new foods to your baby as single ingredient purees before including them in combination purees. This is especially important for foods such as fish that may cause an allergic reaction.

Also Good With: Adding 2 teaspoons of grass-fed butter or olive oil to this puree not only adds a healthy fat into your baby's diet but also enhances the salmon flavor.

CLOSER LOOK
Cloves

Ground cloves (not to be confused with clove oil, which shouldn't be used with little ones under two years old) is one of my favorite spices to add to baby purees. Not only does it add a bold yet warm and sweet taste to a wide variety of fruits and vegetables, but it also has some great medicinal properties. Ground cloves can help to aid digestion, soothe sore teeth and gums, and boost the immune system to help fight off colds, the flu, and a cough. Since this is a powerful spice, you only need a small amount to flavor any puree or dish and to reap the healthy benefits.

PEAR PUREES

Prep Time 5 minutes
Cook Time 15–20 minutes
Yield about 20–30 oz (560–850 g)
Storage 3 days in fridge or
2 months in freezer

Pears are a great way to introduce your baby to the natural sweetness of whole foods. These gems are full of fiber, potassium, and vitamin C, which are all vital for a healthy heart, immune system, and digestive tract.

 ### PEAR AND CINNAMON PUREE *(shown opposite)*
While it's tempting to stand over the stove and take frequent spoonfuls of this puree to taste test, try to leave your baby at least a small sample of this delicious snack.

Ingredients:
- 4 pears, cored, peeled, and chopped
- ½ teaspoon ground cinnamon
- ⅓ cup (80 ml) water

1 Put the pears, cinnamon, and water in a medium saucepan. Cover and cook over medium-low heat for 15 minutes, stirring occasionally, or until pears are tender. Let cool slightly.
2 Transfer to a blender or food processor and puree until smooth.

  ### variation | PEAR, BANANA, MANGO, AND NUTMEG PUREE
Make the puree using the main recipe (above), using ½ teaspoon ground nutmeg instead of the cinnamon. After 10 minutes of cooking, add 2 peeled and chopped bananas; 1 pitted, peeled, and chopped mango; and another ½ cup (120 ml) water. Cook for 5 minutes, then cool and puree as instructed in the main recipe.

Also Good With: This puree is amazing mixed in with a big spoonful or two of Greek yogurt.

 ### variation | PEAR, AVOCADO, AND KIWI PUREE
Make the puree using the main recipe (above), omitting the cinnamon, and cook for 10 minutes. Add 1 pitted and peeled avocado and 4 peeled and chopped kiwi fruits to the blender with the pears, and puree as instructed in the main recipe.

PEAR AND CINNAMON PUREE, PAGE 34

variation | PEAR, STRAWBERRY, AND FLAXSEED PUREE

Make the puree using the main recipe (page 34), omitting the cinnamon and adding 2 cups (300 g) hulled and chopped strawberries and ½ tablespoon flaxseeds, and increasing the water to ⅔ cup (160 ml). Cook over medium heat for 15 minutes, stirring every couple of minutes to prevent the strawberries from burning. Let cool and puree as instructed in the main recipe.

variation | COMFORTING TURKEY DINNER WITH CRANBERRIES, PEAR, AND QUINOA PUREE

Make the puree using the main recipe (page 34)—adding cinnamon is optional—adding 1 cup cubed turkey breast and 1 cup (100 g) fresh or frozen cranberries to the pan. Increase the liquid to 1½ cups (360 ml) low-sodium chicken broth or water and cook over medium heat for 15 minutes, stirring occasionally, or until the turkey is cooked all the way through. Cool and puree as instructed in the main recipe. Add 1 cup (180 g) cooked quinoa to the puree for a chunky puree, or add to the blender and puree for an additional 20 seconds for a smooth puree, adding additional liquid in ¼ cup (60 ml) increments if needed.

Also Good With: ½ teaspoon ground cloves, cinnamon, or nutmeg (or a mixture of all three) will make this puree a taste sensation!

CLOSER LOOK
Ripe Pears

In peak season pears may be so ripe that you don't have to cook them before you puree them. The ripest pear will smell sweet and have a yellow color that may be accentuated with a rosy blush. Look for fruit that's firm and free of bruises and other blemishes.

BANANA PUREES

Prep Time 5 minutes
Cook Time 20 minutes
Yield about 15–25 oz (425–700 g)
Storage 4 days in fridge or
3 months in freezer

Bananas are one amazing on-the-go snack—they even come in their own handy wrapper and are perfect mashed for a first food. Since they are full of potassium and fiber, you will be thrilled when they become one of your baby's (and the entire family's) favorite foods.

BANANA AND CLOVE PUREE *(shown on page 41)*

The taste bar gets raised a couple of notches when bananas are quickly roasted, leaving a puree so decadent that parents want to eat it too.

Ingredients:
- 4 bananas, peeled and cut lengthwise
- ¼ teaspoon ground cloves
- 1 cup (240 ml) water, formula, or breastmilk

1 Preheat the oven to 400°F (200°C). Line a baking sheet with aluminum foil, parchment paper, or a silicon mat. Lay the bananas on the baking sheet and sprinkle with the cloves. Bake for 20 minutes or until the bananas begin to brown. Let cool slightly.

2 Transfer the bananas and liquid to a blender or food processor, and puree until smooth, adding additional liquid in ¼ cup (60 ml) increments if needed.

variation | BANANA, APRICOT, PEACH, AND CHIA SEED PUREE

Make the puree using the main recipe (above), omitting the cloves and adding 3 pitted and chopped apricots and 2 peeled, pitted, and chopped peaches to the baking sheet. Bake for 20–25 minutes or until the bananas are just brown and the peaches and apricots are tender. Let cool and puree as instructed in the main recipe, adding 1 tablespoon chia seeds to the blender.

variation | BANANA, BERRY, CARROT, AND CINNAMON PUREE

Preheat the oven to 400°F (200°C). Start by roasting 3 cups (390 g) chopped carrots on a baking sheet for 30 minutes, stirring halfway through. Add the 4 bananas, sprinkle with 1 teaspoon ground cinnamon, and bake for another 10 minutes. Add 1 cup (150 g) mixed berries (blueberries, strawberries, blackberries, or raspberries all work) and cook for another 5–10 minutes or until the banana is just golden and berries are bursting. Let cool and puree as instructed in the main recipe (above).

AVOCADO PUREES

Prep Time 5 minutes
Cook Time none
Yield about 3–8 oz (85–225 g)
Storage 1 day in fridge or
3 months in freezer

Avocados are quite possibly the world's best food for babies—full of essential healthy fat that helps boost brain and body development—and they have a creamy texture that is super easy for any tiny eater to fall in love with.

AVOCADO AND COCONUT MILK PUREE *(shown on pages 39 and 41)*
A splash of canned coconut milk gives this puree a slight tropical flavor and a creamy texture that is perfect for babies just starting their culinary adventures.

Ingredients:
- ¼ avocado, peeled and pitted
- 1 tablespoon canned coconut milk

Smash the avocado with the back of a spoon or with a fork on a clean cutting board. Drizzle with coconut milk and continue to mix until smooth and creamy. Serve immediately for best results. If freezing or keeping until later in the day, add ¼ teaspoon of lemon or lime juice, stir, and freeze immediately (the puree will last a couple of hours and then will start to brown).

variation | AVOCADO, PINEAPPLE, AND BANANA PUREE
Place ¼ avocado, peeled and pitted, along with ½ peeled banana and ¼ cup (35 g) canned or fresh pineapple chunks in a blender or food processor, and puree until smooth. Serve immediately for best results.

AVOCADO AND COCONUT MILK PUREE, PAGE 38

variation | AVOCADO, BLUEBERRY, OAT, AND VANILLA PUREE

Place ¼ avocado, peeled and pitted, along with ½ cup (70 g) blueberries, ¼ cup (45 g) cooked oats, and ¼ teaspoon vanilla extract in a blender or food processor. Puree until smooth, adding water or coconut milk in ¼ cup (60 ml) increments if needed. This puree does freeze well, so serve or freeze immediately for best results.

variation | AVOCADO, MANGO, PRUNE, AND MINT PUREE

Pour boiling water over 2 dried prunes in a small bowl. Let the prunes plump up for 10 minutes. Place ¼ avocado, peeled and pitted, along with ¼ cup (35 g) peeled and chopped mango, the soaked prunes, and 3 mint leaves in a blender or food processor, and puree until smooth. Serve or store as for the variation above.

BLUEBERRY PUREES

Prep Time 5 minutes
Cook Time 5–15 minutes
Yield about 15–20 oz (425–560 g)
Storage 3 days in fridge or
2 months in freezer

If there is one fruit to make sure your little one loves from the start, it's blueberries. They are full of antioxidants, fiber, and vitamin A, which are all essential for your baby's growth and development, and they make a great on-the-go snack for older toddlers.

 ### BLUEBERRY AND CINNAMON PUREE *(shown opposite)*

Quickly steaming blueberries helps their outer skin puree into a smooth consistency. Cinnamon adds an extra sweetness.

Ingredients:
- 2 cups (280 g) fresh or frozen blueberries
- 1 eating apple, peeled, cored, and chopped
- ½ teaspoon ground cinnamon

1 Fill a medium saucepan with about 2 inches (5 cm) of water and heat on medium until the water begins to boil. Place the blueberries and apple in a steamer basket over the boiling water, cover, and cook for 5 minutes or until just tender. Let cool slightly. Reserve steamer water.
2 Transfer the blueberries, apple, and cinnamon to a blender or food processor, and puree until smooth, adding reserved water in ¼ cup (60 ml) increments if needed.

 ### variation | BLUEBERRY, PURPLE CARROT, AND NUTMEG PUREE

Prepare the steamer basket as instructed in the main recipe (above) and cook 3 peeled and chopped purple carrots and the apple for 10 minutes. Add the blueberries and cook for another 5 minutes. Let cool and puree as instructed in the main recipe, adding ¼ teaspoon ground nutmeg to the blender.

 ### variation | BLUEBERRY, SPINACH, PEACH, AND BASIL PUREE

Make the puree using the main recipe (above), omitting the cinnamon and adding 2 cups (450 g) chopped peaches (fresh or frozen) and 1 packed cup (30 g) spinach to the steamer basket in that order. Cook, cool, and puree as instructed in the main recipe, adding 3 basil leaves to the blender.

Also Good With: This recipe is great with a spoonful of protein-rich Greek yogurt stirred in right before serving.

variation | BLUEBERRY, BEEF, BEET, AND MINT PUREE
Prepare the steamer basket as instructed in the main recipe (page 40)
and cook 4 oz (115 g) sirloin steak chunks and 2 peeled, trimmed, and
finely chopped beets for 10 minutes. Add the blueberries as instructed
in the main recipe and cook for another 5 minutes or until the beef is
cooked all the way through. Let cool and puree as instructed in the
main recipe, adding 3 mint leaves to the blender.

BLUEBERRY AND CINNAMON PUREE, PAGE 40

AVOCADO AND COCONUT MILK PUREE, PAGE 38

BANANA AND CLOVE PUREE, PAGE 37

PEACH PUREES

Prep Time 5 minutes
Cook Time 10 minutes
Yield about 20–25 oz (560–700 g)
Storage 3 days in fridge or
2 months in freezer

Peaches are packed with vitamins A and C as well as fiber, which promotes healthy bone growth and supports your baby's immune system. These fruits are also packed with flavor—a ripe, juicy, and sweet flavor that is like a spoonful of sunshine for your baby to enjoy.

 ## PEACH AND VANILLA PUREE *(shown opposite)*
This puree is going to be a taste explosion for baby—bright, sweet, syrupy goodness—it's like a baby version of peach pie!

Ingredients:
* 4 peaches (fresh or frozen), peeled, pitted, and chopped
* 1 cup (240 ml) water
* ½ teaspoon vanilla extract

1 Put the peaches and water in a medium saucepan and heat over medium heat for 10 minutes or until the peaches are tender and can be cut with the back of a spoon.
2 Use a slotted spoon to transfer the peaches to a blender or food processor, reserving the peach water. Add the vanilla extract and puree until smooth, adding reserved water in ¼ cup (60 ml) increments if needed.

 ## variation | PEACH, PLUM, AND BLUEBERRY PUREE
Make the puree using the main recipe (above)—vanilla is optional—adding 3 pitted and chopped plums and 1 cup (140 g) blueberries and increasing the water to 1½ cups (360 ml). Cook and puree as instructed in the main recipe. Add 1 tablespoon of yogurt to the puree before serving. This puree is not suitable for freezing once the yogurt has been added.

Also Good With: Add ground cinnamon, cloves, ginger, nutmeg, or a mixture of spices for extra flavor and nutrients.

 ## variation | PEACH, CARROT, APRICOT, AND QUINOA PUREE
Make the puree using the main recipe (above), adding 3 peeled and chopped carrots and 3 pitted and chopped apricots (fresh or frozen) and increasing the water to 2 cups (480 ml). Cook for 15 minutes or until the carrots are tender. Continue as instructed in the main recipe, adding 1 cup (180 g) cooked quinoa to the blender as you puree (or fold it through for a chunky puree).

variation | PEACH, MANGO, WILD SALMON, AND CILANTRO PUREE

Make the puree using the main recipe (page 42), adding 1 peeled, pitted, and chopped mango and 1 skinned and chopped 6 oz (175 g) salmon fillet, and increasing the water in the pan until all the ingredients are covered. Bring to a boil over high heat, reduce heat to low, and simmer for 10–15 minutes or until the salmon is cooked all the way through. Using a slotted spoon, transfer the ingredients into a blender, reserving the water, along with 1 tablespoon chopped cilantro. Puree until smooth, adding additional reserved water in ¼ cup (60 ml) increments if needed.

Combination Purees: Always introduce new foods to your baby as single ingredient purees before including them in combination purees. This is especially important for foods such as fish that may cause an allergic reaction.

PEACH AND VANILLA PUREE, PAGE 42

SWEET POTATO PUREES

Prep Time 5 minutes
Cook Time 15–20 minutes
Yield about 25–30 oz (700–850 g)
Storage 4 days in fridge or 3 months in freezer

Sweet potatoes are a great first food for your baby. Not only are they packed with potassium, beta carotene, calcium, and fiber—which help promote a healthy digestive tract—but their sweet taste is usually a win too!

SWEET POTATO AND CURRY PUREE

Gently steaming sweet potatoes makes a crisper-tasting puree and takes less then half the time of roasting. I love to add a teaspoon of deep spices to this puree, such as curry and coriander.

Ingredients:
- 3 medium sweet potatoes, peeled and chopped
- 1 teaspoon mild curry powder
- 1 cup (240 ml) low- or no-sodium chicken or vegetable broth, reserved steamer water, breastmilk, or formula

1 Fill a medium saucepan with about 2 inches (5 cm) of water. Heat on medium until the water begins to boil. Place the sweet potatoes in a steamer basket over boiling water. Cover and cook for 15–20 minutes or until you can easily prick the potatoes with a fork. Let cool slightly.
2 Transfer the sweet potatoes to a blender or food processor, and add the curry powder and liquid. Puree until smooth, adding additional liquid in ¼ cup (60 ml) increments if needed.

variation | SWEET POTATO, PEAR, AND THYME PUREE

Make the puree using the main recipe (above), omitting the curry powder and adding 2 cored and chopped pears (peeling optional) and 1 teaspoon freshly chopped thyme to the steamer basket. Cover, cook, cool, and puree as instructed in the main recipe.

Also Good With: ½ cup (30 g) chopped kale added during the steaming process is a delicious and nutritious addition.

variation | SWEET POTATO, APPLE, RED BELL PEPPER, AND CORIANDER PUREE

Make the puree using the main recipe (page 44), omitting the curry powder and adding 1 cored, peeled, and chopped eating apple and 1 deseeded and chopped red bell pepper to the steamer basket in that order. Cover, cook, and cool as instructed in the main recipe. Add ½ teaspoon coriander to the blender with the rest of the ingredients and puree as instructed in the main recipe.

variation | SWEET POTATO, ACORN SQUASH, AND MILLET PUREE *(shown below)*

Make the puree using the main recipe (page 44), omitting the curry powder and adding ½ deseeded, peeled, and chopped acorn squash to the steamer basket. Cover, cook, cool, and puree as instructed in the main recipe. Fold in 1 cup (60 g) cooked millet for a chunky puree, or add millet to the blender and puree for a smooth puree.

Also Good With: 1 teaspoon fresh chopped cilantro added to the blender right before pureeing for an exciting taste kick!

SWEET POTATO, ACORN SQUASH, AND MILLET PUREE, SEE ABOVE

BUTTERNUT SQUASH PUREES

Prep Time 5 minutes
Cook Time 1 hour
Yield about 25–30 oz (700–850 g)
Storage 4 days in fridge or 3 months in freezer

Roasting butternut squash brings out the natural rich caramel flavor, intensifying the sweetness that babies just can't resist. This type of squash has a huge amount of beta carotene, fiber, and vitamins A and E, which help to support your baby's immune system, skin, and bones.

BUTTERNUT SQUASH AND OLIVE OIL PUREE *(shown opposite)*

While the cook time is 60 minutes, the hands-on time is only 5 minutes, leaving you with 55 minutes to yourself.

Ingredients:
- 1 medium butternut squash, cut in half and deseeded
- 2 teaspoons olive oil
- 1 cup (240 ml) low- or no-sodium chicken or vegetable broth, water, formula, or breastmilk

1 Preheat the oven to 400°F (200°C) and line a baking sheet with aluminum foil, parchment paper, or a silicon mat. Place the squash, skin side down, on the baking sheet and drizzle with the oil. Bake for 45–60 minutes or until the flesh is tender and can be pricked with a fork. Let cool slightly.
2 Scrape the flesh away from the skin and discard the skin. Transfer the squash and liquid to a blender or food processor, and puree until smooth, adding additional liquid in ¼ cup (60 ml) increments if needed.

variation | BUTTERNUT SQUASH, YELLOW SQUASH, AND THYME PUREE

Place half a deseeded butternut squash and 3 small, trimmed yellow summer squashes cut in half lengthwise on a lined baking sheet. Bake in an oven preheated as in the main recipe (above) for 30 minutes. After baking, remove the yellow squash and set aside to cool. Bake the butternut squash for another 15–20 minutes or until the flesh is tender and can be pricked with a fork. Let cool slightly. Scoop the butternut squash flesh away from the skin and discard. Place the butternut squash and yellow squash along with ½ tablespoon of chopped fresh thyme and liquid into a blender or food processor, and puree as instructed in the main recipe.

Also Good With: I love adding 1 cup (60 g) cooked barley to this puree for some additional fiber and magnesium. You can leave it chunky or add to the blender with the squash for a smooth puree.

variation | BUTTERNUT SQUASH, SWEET POTATO, PEAR, AND SAGE PUREE

Make the puree using the main recipe (page 46), but use only half the butternut squash (olive oil is optional) and add 1 sweet potato, pricked with a fork several times, to the lined baking sheet. Bake for 30 minutes, then add 2 cored, peeled, and chopped pears to the baking sheet and cook for another 15 minutes or until squash and sweet potato are tender. Let cool slightly, then peel the squash and sweet potato as instructed in the main recipe. Add all the ingredients, plus 2 chopped sage leaves and the liquid to the blender or food processor, and puree as instructed in the main recipe.

CARROT AND CUMIN PUREE, PAGE 48

BROCCOLI AND CHIVE PUREE, PAGE 49

BUTTERNUT SQUASH AND OLIVE OIL PUREE, PAGE 46

CARROT PUREES

Prep Time 5 minutes
Cook Time 10 minutes
Yield about 20–25 oz (560–700 g)
Storage 4 days in fridge or 3 months in freezer

If you are looking to get some vitamin A into your baby, carrot puree is the clear winner. One serving of this sweet root vegetable has over 200 percent of their daily vitamin A needs, which helps your baby's immune system, skin, eyes, and bones.

 CARROT AND CUMIN PUREE *(shown on page 47)*

Homemade carrot puree is so tasty that you and your baby will be fighting over the last spoonful. Adding a pinch of cumin, nutmeg, cloves, or turmeric brings out the carrot's earthy flavor.

Ingredients:
- 1 lb (450 g) carrots, peeled, trimmed, and chopped
- ½ teaspoon ground cumin
- 1 cup (240 ml) reserved steamer water, formula, or breastmilk

1 Fill a medium saucepan with about 2 inches (5 cm) of water and heat on medium until the water begins to boil. Place the carrots in a steamer basket over the boiling water. Cover and cook for 10 minutes or until just tender. Let cool slightly. Reserve steamer water.
2 Transfer the carrots to a blender or food processor, then add the cumin and liquid. Puree until smooth, adding additional liquid in ¼ cup (60 ml) increments if needed.

 ## variation | CARROT, PARSNIP, MANGO, AND CHIA SEED PUREE

Make the puree using the main recipe (above), omitting the cumin and adding 1 peeled, trimmed, and chopped parsnip to the steamer basket, and cook for 10 minutes. Add 1 peeled and pitted mango and cook for another 5 minutes. Transfer all the ingredients, along with 1 teaspoon chia seeds and the liquid, to the blender and puree as instructed in the main recipe.

 ## variation | SPICED CARROT PUREE WITH COCONUT MILK

Make the puree using the main recipe (above), omitting the cumin and adding 1 large peeled and chopped sweet potato to the steamer basket and cook for 15 minutes or until the potato is tender. Transfer to the blender, adding in ½ cup (70 g) cooked, drained chickpeas; ½ cup (120 ml) canned coconut milk; and ½ teaspoon ground turmeric. Puree as instructed in the main recipe, adding either reserved water or coconut milk as needed.

BROCCOLI PUREES

Prep Time 5 minutes
Cook Time 15 minutes
Yield about 12–20 oz (350–560 g)
Storage 4 days in fridge or 3 months in freezer

Broccoli isn't my favorite vegetable, but that didn't stop me from introducing both of my girls to broccoli puree when they were babies. Broccoli is a powerhouse food loaded with vitamin C, soluble fiber, and folate and is an all-around superfood.

BROCCOLI AND CHIVE PUREE *(shown on page 47)*

Nowadays, you can find Ellie pulling the kitchen stool up to the fridge, with Parker on her heels, as they co-conspire on stealing broccoli chunks out of the fridge for an impromptu morning snack.

Ingredients:
- 2 cups (120 g) broccoli florets
- 1 small white potato, peeled and quartered
- 1 teaspoon chives, finely chopped
- ½ cup (120 ml) reserved steamer water, formula, or breastmilk

1. Fill a medium saucepan with about 2 inches (5 cm) of water and heat on medium until the water begins to boil. Place the broccoli and potato in a steamer basket over the boiling water. Cover and cook for 12–15 minutes or until just tender. Let cool slightly. Reserve steamer water.
2. Transfer the broccoli and potato to a blender or food processor, and add the chives and liquid. Puree until smooth, adding additional liquid in ¼ cup (60 ml) increments if needed.

variation | BROCCOLI, ZUCCHINI, CAULIFLOWER, AND PARSLEY PUREE

Make the puree using the main recipe (above), omitting the potato and chives and adding 1 trimmed and chopped zucchini and 1 cup (75 g) cauliflower to the steamer basket. Cook for 15 minutes, then cool and puree as instructed in the main recipe, adding 1 tablespoon finely chopped parsley to the blender.

variation | BROCCOLI, PEAR, PEA, AND MINT PUREE

Make the puree using the main recipe (above), omitting the potato and chives and adding 2 deseeded and chopped pears and 1 cup (160 g) shelled peas (fresh or frozen) to the steamer basket. Cook, cool, and puree as instructed in the main recipe, adding 4 chopped mint leaves to the blender.

GREEN BEAN PUREES

Prep Time 5 minutes
Cook Time 15 minutes
Yield about 20–30 oz (560–850 g)
Storage 3–4 days in fridge or 2–3 months in freezer

Green beans make a great mild puree that is filled with calcium, manganese, and vitamins K and C. During the cold and flu season, I keep reusable pouches full of this puree for a quick nutritional boost for the girls.

 GREEN BEAN AND CILANTRO PUREE *(shown opposite)*

A quick steam is all that is needed for a mild and creamy bean puree without any bitterness. I pair this with sharp cilantro for a fun new taste for your little one.

Ingredients:
- 1 lb (450 g) green beans, trimmed
- 2 teaspoons fresh cilantro, chopped
- ½ cup (120 ml) low- or no-sodium chicken or vegetable broth, reserved steamer water, formula, or breastmilk

1 Fill a medium saucepan with about 2 inches (5 cm) of water. Heat on medium until the water begins to boil. Place the green beans in a steamer basket over the boiling water, cover, and cook for 10 minutes or until just tender. Let cool slightly. Reserve steamer water.
2 Transfer the beans to a blender or food processor, and add the cilantro and liquid. Puree until smooth, adding additional liquid in ¼ cup (60 ml) increments if needed.

 variation | GREEN BEAN, PEA, ASPARAGUS, APPLE, AND DATE PUREE

Make the puree using the main recipe (above), omitting the cilantro and adding 1 cup (160 g) shelled peas; 1 cup (115 g) chopped asparagus; and 1 cored, peeled, and chopped sweet eating apple to the steamer basket. Cook for 10–15 minutes or until the apple is tender. Reserve steamer water. Meanwhile, in a small bowl, pour boiling water over 4 pitted dates and let steep for 10 minutes. Transfer all the ingredients to a blender or food processor, and puree as instructed in the main recipe.

variation | THAI CHICKEN AND GREEN BEAN PUREE

Make the puree using the main recipe (page 50), omitting the cilantro and adding 1 cubed boneless skinless chicken breast to the steamer basket on top of green beans. Cook for 15 minutes or until chicken is cooked all the way through. Let cool slightly. Transfer the beans, chicken, and liquid to the blender and add ½ minced garlic clove, 1 teaspoon freshly grated ginger, and ½ teaspoon mild curry powder and puree as instructed in the main recipe.

Also Good With: 1 cup (135 g) cooked brown rice stirred through this puree adds some extra fiber and texture.

GREEN BEAN AND CILANTRO PUREE, PAGE 50

ASPARAGUS AND MINT PUREE, PAGE 53

ASPARAGUS PUREES

Prep Time 5 minutes
Cook Time 10 minutes
Yield about 20–30 oz (560–850 g)
Storage 4 days in fridge or
3 months in freezer

Ohhh snap! Asparagus puree is where it is at! Asparagus is filled with vitamin C, fiber, and folic acid. These nutrients are vital to regulate bone development and support cardiovascular function in your baby's body.

 ## ASPARAGUS AND MINT PUREE *(shown opposite)*

I wasn't a big asparagus puree fan until I mixed it with some mint, and then I was hooked. Light and playful, this puree will leave your baby wanting more, more, more!

Ingredients:
- 1 lb (450 g) asparagus, chopped (fresh or frozen)
- 4 fresh mint leaves
- ½ cup (120 ml) reserved steamer water, formula, or breastmilk

1 Fill a medium saucepan with about 2 inches (5 cm) of water and heat on medium until the water begins to boil. Place the asparagus in a steamer basket over the boiling water, cover, and cook for 10 minutes or until just tender. Let cool slightly. Reserve steamer water.
2 Transfer the asparagus to a blender or food processor, and add the mint and liquid. Puree until smooth, adding additional liquid in ¼ cup (60 ml) increments if needed.

 ## variation | ASPARAGUS, AVOCADO, AND LEMON PUREE

Steam the asparagus using the main recipe (above) and let cool. Transfer to the blender, adding 1 ripe, peeled, and pitted avocado; the juice from ½ a lemon; and the liquid. Puree as instructed in the main recipe.

 ## variation | ASPARAGUS, PEACH, WHITE FISH, AND RICOTTA PUREE

Prepare the steamer basket as instructed in the main recipe (above) and add 2 peeled and pitted peaches, then an 8 oz (225 g) skinned and deboned white fish fillet (tilapia or cod) on top. Steam for 10 minutes or until fish is cooked all the way through. Transfer to the blender and puree as instructed in the main recipe. Swirl in 1 teaspoon ricotta cheese before serving.

RED BELL PEPPER PUREES

Prep Time 5 minutes
Cook Time 10 minutes
Yield about 14–20 oz (400–560 g)
Storage 4 days in fridge or 3 months in freezer

Bell pepper might seem like an interesting choice for a first puree but when gently steamed and pureed, it makes a smooth, creamy, and almost fruity puree. High in vitamins C and E, beta carotene, and folate, these sweet bell peppers help to develop skin and bones.

RED BELL PEPPER AND THYME PUREE *(shown opposite)*

I like to serve this puree warm for baby and with a spoonful of crème fraîche for me! For a wonderful first finger food, toss this puree in with small-shaped pasta.

Ingredients:

- 3 red bell peppers, deseeded and chopped
- 1 small white potato, peeled and quartered
- ½ teaspoon thyme leaves, chopped
- ¼ cup (60 ml) reserved steamer water, low- or no-sodium vegetable or chicken broth, formula, or breastmilk

1 Fill a medium saucepan with about 2 inches (5 cm) of water and heat on medium until the water begins to boil. Place the red bell pepper and potato in a steamer basket over the boiling water, then cover and cook for 7 minutes or until just tender. Let cool slightly. Reserve steamer water.

2 Transfer the red bell pepper and potato to a blender or food processor, and add the thyme leaves and the reserved water or other liquid. Puree until smooth, adding additional liquid in ¼ cup (60 ml) increments if needed.

variation | RED BELL PEPPER, CARROT, WHITE BEAN, AND PARSLEY PUREE

Make the puree using the main recipe (above), omitting the potato and thyme and adding 3 peeled, trimmed, and chopped carrots and ½ cup (70 g) cooked, rinsed, and drained white beans (such as cannellini beans or navy beans) into the steamer basket. Cook for 10 minutes or until the carrots are tender. Reserve steamer water. Transfer all ingredients to the blender, adding 1 tablespoon chopped parsley and ½ cup (120 ml) reserved steamer water. Puree as instructed in the main recipe.

variation | THAI RED BELL PEPPER AND BEEF PUREE WITH GINGER

Make the puree using the main recipe (page 54), omitting the potato and thyme and adding in 1 peeled, seeded, and chopped mango and 8 oz (225 g) chopped beef sirloin. Cook for 10–15 minutes or until the beef is cooked all the way through. Reserve steamer water. Let cool slightly. Transfer to the blender and add ½ teaspoon freshly grated ginger and ½ cup (120 ml) steamer water or low- or no-sodium beef broth, and puree as instructed in the main recipe.

....

Also Good With: This puree is fantastic served chunky over some cooked brown rice for older babies. Delish!

....

Salt in Broth: Broth is a great gut-healthy food. However, store-bought broths can contain high levels of salt. Choose a low-sodium broth, or better yet, make your own broth to add to your baby's purees.

RED BELL PEPPER AND THYME PUREE, PAGE 54

BEET PUREES

Prep Time 5 minutes
Cook Time 20 minutes
Yield about 20–30 oz (560–850 g)
Storage 4 days in fridge or
3 months in freezer

Besides giving your baby a visual POW, beets are high in calcium, potassium, and carbohydrates, which help boost baby's stamina. The perfect puree to support your baby as they crawl, stand, fall, walk, and fall some more.

 BEET AND MINT PUREE *(shown opposite)*

When you pair this beautiful beet puree with mint, you get a mild puree with a refreshing zing—perfectly balanced for a baby's first food.

Ingredients:
* 5 red or yellow beets, peeled and chopped
* 4 mint leaves, finely chopped
* 1 cup (240 ml) reserved water, formula, or breastmilk

1 Fill a medium saucepan with about 2 inches (5 cm) of water and heat on medium until the water begins to boil. Place the beets in a steamer basket over the boiling water. Cover and cook for 15–20 minutes or until just tender. Let cool slightly. Reserve steamer water.
2 Transfer the beets to a blender or food processor, then add the mint leaves and liquid. Puree until smooth, adding additional liquid in ¼ cup (60 ml) increments if needed.

 variation | BEET, STRAWBERRY, CLOVE, AND YOGURT PUREE

Make the puree using the main recipe (above), omitting the mint and cooking for 15 minutes. Add 2 cups (300 g) hulled strawberries and cook for another 5 minutes. Let cool slightly, reserving the steamer water. Add ingredients to the blender along with ½ teaspoon ground cloves and puree as instructed in the main recipe. Stir in 1 tablespoon plain yogurt to every 2 oz (60 g) of puree right before serving.

Also Good With: To upgrade this puree to a healthy afternoon snack for older toddlers, swirl in the yogurt with ½ tablespoon honey and 1 tablespoon finely chopped almonds (see Nuts and Seeds box, page 115).

 variation | BEET, CARROT, SWEET POTATO, AND CINNAMON PUREE

Make the puree using the main recipe (above), omitting the mint and adding 3 peeled, chopped carrots and ½ peeled and chopped sweet potato to the steamer basket. Let cool and puree as instructed in the main recipe, adding ½ teaspoon ground cinnamon to the blender.

variation | YELLOW BEET, FENNEL, APRICOT, AND SAGE PUREE

Make the puree using the main recipe (page 56), omitting the mint, using only yellow beets, and adding 1 trimmed and chopped fennel bulb and 3 dried, fresh, or frozen apricots to the steamer basket. Cook for 15 minutes or until the beets are tender. Let cool and puree as instructed in the main recipe, adding 3 chopped sage leaves to the blender.

Also Good With: Adding ½ cup (30 g) cooked millet is a great way to make this into a chunky puree filled with extra protein and iron.

BEET AND MINT PUREE, PAGE 56

PUMPKIN PUREES

Prep Time 5 minutes
Cook Time 1 hour
Yield about 20–30 oz (560–850 g)
Storage 4 days in fridge or
3 months in freezer

Ellie started her culinary adventure at the tail end of the pumpkin season. It was a good thing I went a little crazy in the kitchen one night and made over 140 oz (4 kg) pumpkin puree, because in the blink of an eye, all of my frozen pumpkin back-stock was gone.

 ## PUMPKIN AND NUTMEG PUREE

If your baby is lucky enough to be eating purees during pumpkin season—get at it! This puree will not disappoint.

Ingredients:

- ½ pie pumpkin, deseeded
- ½ teaspoon ground nutmeg
- ½ cup (120 ml) water, low- or no-sodium vegetable or chicken broth, formula, or breastmilk

1 Preheat the oven to 400°F (200°C). Place the pumpkin in a baking dish, skin side up, and fill with 1 inch (2.5 cm) of water. Bake for 45–60 minutes or until you can easily prick the skin of the pumpkin with a fork. Let cool slightly.

2 Scrape out the pumpkin flesh and place in a blender or food processor. Add the nutmeg and liquid, and puree until smooth, adding additional liquid in ¼ cup (60 ml) increments if needed.

 ## variation | ROASTED FALL VEGETABLES WITH CHICKEN AND THYME PUREE *(shown opposite)*

Prepare the pumpkin as instructed in the main recipe (above), omitting the water and nutmeg and adding 1 peeled and halved parsnip and 1 sweet potato pricked several times with a fork. Put 8 oz (225 g) chicken breast or thigh meat inside an aluminum foil packet and add this to the baking dish too. Bake for 45 minutes and check all ingredients for doneness. The chicken should be cooked all the way through, and the sweet potato and pumpkin should be easily pricked with a fork. Cook for an additional 10–15 minutes if needed. Let cool slightly, then scrape out the pumpkin and sweet potato flesh as instructed in the main recipe. Transfer all ingredients along with 1 cup (240 ml) liquid and ½ tablespoon chopped thyme leaves to a blender or food processor, and puree as instructed in the main recipe, adding additional liquid in ¼ cup (60 ml) increments if needed.

variation | PUMPKIN, PEAR, AND BANANA PUREE WITH YOGURT AND CINNAMON

Make the puree using the main recipe (page 58), omitting the nutmeg and cooking for 45 minutes. Remove the pumpkin from the baking dish, drain the water, and add 2 cored and quartered pears and 2 peeled and halved bananas. Bake for another 10 minutes or until the banana is just browning. Let cool slightly. Scrape out the pumpkin flesh and transfer all ingredients to the blender along with 2 teaspoons ground cinnamon and the liquid. Puree as instructed in the main recipe. Swirl in 1 tablespoon yogurt before serving.

variation | PUMPKIN AND PEACH PUREE WITH OATS

Bake the pumpkin as instructed in the main recipe (page 58), but only cook for 30 minutes. Add 2 pitted peaches to the baking dish and more water if needed (there should be roughly 1 inch/2.5 cm in the dish). Bake for 20 minutes or until the peaches and pumpkin can be pricked with a fork. Let cool slightly. Scrape out pumpkin flesh and transfer all the ingredients, including the ½ cup (120 ml) liquid, to the blender and puree as instructed in the main recipe. Add 2 cups (200 g) cooked oats to the blender and pulse until you have your desired consistency, adding additional liquid in ¼ cup (60 ml) increments if needed.

ROASTED FALL VEGETABLES WITH CHICKEN AND THYME PUREE, PAGE 58

NEXT STEPS

Now that your baby has the basic purees down, it's time to up the ante. Grains, meat, and fish are all amazing foods to add to babies' meals early on. Not only do they provide essential nutritional compounds, but they introduce your little one to new taste and texture experiences. Served chunky or pureed, these purees are surely going to be a grand slam with your tiny eater.

QUINOA PUREES 62 • MILLET PUREES 64 • LENTIL PUREES 66 • OAT PUREES 67 • CHICKEN PUREES 70 • BEEF PUREES 72 • SALMON PUREES 74 • WHITE FISH PUREES 76

QUINOA PUREES

Prep Time 5 minutes
Cook Time 20 minutes
Yield about 15–20 oz (425–560 g)
Storage 3 days in fridge or
2 months in freezer

This gluten-free grain is full of healthy fiber, calcium, and iron and is a great first grain for baby. Quinoa is a complete protein that purees to a smooth texture for first purees. Left whole, it has a soft, fluffy bite for a chunkier meal.

QUINOA, PEAR, AND CINNAMON PUREE

This simple quinoa puree is full of sweet pears and cinnamon that makes a perfect breakfast dish on a cold morning—pureed for your baby and left as is for you!

Ingredients:

- 1 cup (180 g) quinoa, rinsed and drained
- 2 cups (480 ml) water or low- or no-sodium chicken or vegetable broth
- 2 pears, cored, peeled, and chopped
- 1 teaspoon ground cinnamon

1 Put the quinoa and water in a medium saucepan and bring to a boil over high heat. Reduce heat to medium-low and simmer, covered, for 10 minutes. Add the pears and cinnamon, stir, and cook for another 10 minutes, covered. Remove from heat and let sit, covered, for 5 minutes. Drain any remaining liquid.
2 Transfer all ingredients to a blender or food processor, and puree until you reach your desired consistency, adding additional liquid in ¼ cup (60 ml) increments if needed.

variation | CHUNKY QUINOA, RASPBERRY, AND PEACH PUREE

Make the puree using the main recipe (above), omitting the pears and cinnamon. After cooking quinoa for 10 minutes, add 1 pitted, peeled, and chopped peach and 1 cup (125 g) raspberries (fresh or frozen); stir and cook for another 10 minutes, covered. Continue as instructed in the main recipe. For a chunky puree, pulse a couple of times to incorporate the ingredients, or blend until completely smooth.

Also Good With: Ground cinnamon, cloves, nutmeg, fresh mint, almond extract, and fresh rosemary are all great additions to this recipe to give your baby an extra flavor to enjoy.

 ### variation | QUINOA, AVOCADO, SPINACH, AND CILANTRO PUREE

Make the puree using the main recipe (page 62), omitting the pears and cinnamon. After cooking for 10 minutes, add 1 packed cup (30 g) spinach, then stir and cook for 10 minutes, covered. Continue as instructed in the main recipe, adding 1 pitted, peeled, and chopped avocado and 1 tablespoon chopped fresh cilantro to the blender as you puree.

 ### variation | QUINOA, KALE, ZUCCHINI, AND APPLE PUREE

Make the puree using the main recipe (page 62), omitting the pears and cinnamon. After cooking for 10 minutes, add 2 chopped kale leaves; ½ small chopped zucchini; and 1 cored, peeled, and chopped eating apple. Stir and cook for 10 minutes, covered. Continue as instructed in the main recipe.

 ### variation | QUINOA, BLUEBERRY, CHERRY, AND FLAXSEED PUREE *(shown on page 65)*

Make the puree using the main recipe (page 62), omitting the pears and cinnamon. After cooking for 10 minutes, add 1 cup (150 g) blueberries (fresh or frozen), 1 cup (200 g) pitted cherries, and 1 teaspoon flaxseeds; stir and cook for 10 minutes, covered. Continue as instructed in the main recipe.

MILLET PUREES

Prep Time 5 minutes
Cook Time 25 minutes
Yield about 15–20 oz (425–560 g)
Storage 3 days in fridge or
2 months in freezer

I first came across millet when I started introducing whole grains into Ellie's diet. I love its nutty taste—plus it can be incorporated into almost any puree. Full of potassium, magnesium, and iron, millet is now a staple in our home.

 MILLET, COCONUT MILK, AND CINNAMON PUREE *(shown opposite)*

This warm and creamy puree is perfect for a quick and healthy breakfast for your baby. I have mine with fresh berries and provide just the puree for my baby.

Ingredients:
- 1 cup (185 g) millet, rinsed and drained
- 1½ cups (360 ml) water
- ½ cup (120 ml) full-fat canned coconut milk
- 1 teaspoon ground cinnamon

1 Put all the ingredients in a medium saucepan and bring to a boil. Reduce heat to medium-low and simmer, covered, for 20 minutes. Remove from heat and let sit, covered, for 5 minutes.

2 Transfer to a blender or food processor, and puree until you reach your desired consistency, adding additional liquid in ¼ cup (60 ml) increments if needed. The millet will get thicker as it cools, so I like to add extra coconut milk before serving or freezing.

Also Good With: For extra flavor, add ½ teaspoon vanilla extract and ¼ teaspoon ground ginger during cooking.

 variation | CARROT AND CAULIFLOWER PUREE WITH MILLET AND GINGER

Make the puree using the main recipe (above), omitting the cinnamon, increasing the water to 2½ cups (600 ml), and adding 2 peeled and chopped carrots and 1 cup (75 g) chopped cauliflower. Continue as instructed in the main recipe, adding ½ teaspoon freshly grated ginger to the blender as you puree.

variation | **MILLET, BLACKBERRY, KALE, AND APRICOT PUREE**

Make the puree using the main recipe (page 64), omitting the cinnamon and coconut milk and increasing the water to 2 cups (480 ml). After cooking the millet for 10 minutes, add in 1 cup (140 g) blackberries (fresh or frozen), 1 stem of chopped kale, and 1 cup (200 g) pitted apricots (fresh or frozen); cover and cook for another 10 minutes. Continue as instructed in the main recipe.

Dried Apricots: If you can't find fresh or frozen apricots, you can use 3 dried, pitted apricots. Place the apricots in a small bowl and cover with boiling water. Let sit for 10 minutes, then add them to the blender right before pureeing.

 variation | **MILLET, CORN, YELLOW SQUASH, AND CHIVE PUREE**

Make the puree using the main recipe (page 64), omitting the cinnamon and coconut milk and increasing the water to 2 cups (480 ml). After cooking the millet for 10 minutes, add 1 cup (175 g) corn (fresh or frozen), ½ chopped yellow squash, and 1 tablespoon chopped chives. Cover and cook for another 10 minutes. Continue as instructed in the main recipe.

QUINOA, BLUEBERRY, CHERRY, AND FLAXSEED PUREE, PAGE 63

MILLET, COCONUT MILK, AND CINNAMON PUREE, PAGE 64

LENTIL PUREES

Prep Time 5 minutes
Cook Time 30 minutes
Yield about 15–25 oz (425–700 g)
Storage 3 days in fridge or
2 months in freezer

Not only are lentils a wonderful source of fiber, zinc, calcium, and iron, but when cooked and blended they create a creamy and rich puree that lends itself to bold spices like cumin, paprika, coriander, garam masala, and fresh ginger.

 ### LENTIL, CARROT, AND THYME PUREE *(shown on page 69)*

This lentil puree is a great way to take your baby on a culinary adventure without them ever leaving the high chair!

Ingredients:
- 1 cup (170 g) red lentils, rinsed and drained
- 2½ cups (600 ml) low- or no-sodium chicken or vegetable broth or water
- 2 carrots, peeled and chopped
- ½ teaspoon chopped fresh thyme

1 Put all the ingredients in a medium saucepan and bring to a boil over high heat. Reduce heat to low and simmer for 20–30 minutes, stirring occasionally, adding ¼ cup (60 ml) more of water if needed during cooking, or until the carrots are tender and the lentils are soft. There may be a little excess water left in the pan.
2 Transfer all the ingredients to a blender or food processor, and puree until smooth, adding additional liquid in ¼ cup (60 ml) increments if needed.

 ### variation | LENTIL, PUMPKIN, RICE, CUMIN, AND CINNAMON PUREE

Make the puree using the main recipe (above), omitting the thyme and adding 2 cups (240 g) peeled and chopped pumpkin (butternut squash also works here), ¼ cup (50 g) brown rice, 1 teaspoon ground cumin, and ½ teaspoon ground cinnamon and increasing the water to 3 cups (720 ml). Cook, cool, and puree as instructed in the main recipe.

variation | LENTIL, SPINACH, KALE, BROCCOLI, AND CURRY PUREE

Make the puree using the main recipe (page 66), omitting the thyme and adding 1 cup (30 g) packed spinach, 1 kale leaf, 1 cup (120 g) chopped broccoli, and 1 teaspoon mild curry and increasing the water to 3½ cups (840 ml). Cook, cool, and puree as instructed in the main recipe.

variation | LENTIL, POTATO, APPLE, AND RED CURRY PUREE

Make the puree using the main recipe (page 66), omitting the thyme and adding 1 peeled and chopped white potato, 1 cored and chopped eating apple, and ½ teaspoon mild red curry paste. Cook, cool, and puree as instructed in the main recipe.

OAT PUREES

Prep Time 5 minutes
Cook Time 15 minutes
Yield about 15 oz (425 g)
Storage 3 days in fridge or 2 months in freezer

We eat oats all the time in my house—in purees and porridge, baked in muffins or pancakes, and tossed in smoothies for extra fueling power. Full of fiber and protein, oats help to stabilize blood sugar, promote antioxidant activity, and give you lasting energy.

OAT, PEAR, APPLE, AND CINNAMON PUREE

This is my favorite recipe for a quick and warm breakfast for both baby and toddler, not only because it is healthy and delicious but also because it can be made in less than 15 minutes!

Ingredients:
- ½ cup (45 g) dry rolled oats
- 1 eating apple, cored, peeled, and chopped
- 1 pear, cored, peeled, and chopped
- ½ teaspoon ground cinnamon
- 1½ cups (360 ml) water

1 Put all the ingredients in a medium saucepan and bring to a low boil. Reduce heat to low and simmer for 10–15 minutes or until the apple and pear are tender. Let cool slightly.
2 Transfer all the ingredients to a blender or food processor, and puree until smooth, adding additional liquid in ¼ cup (60 ml) increments until you reach your desired consistency.

variation | OAT, AVOCADO, AND SPINACH PUREE
(shown opposite)

Make the puree using the main recipe (page 67), omitting the apple, pear, and cinnamon and adding 1 cup (30 g) packed spinach. Bring to a boil, then reduce heat and simmer for 10 minutes (there will be a little liquid left in the pan). Puree as instructed in the main recipe, adding 1 pitted and chopped avocado to the blender.

 ### variation | OAT, PEACH, COCONUT MILK, AND GINGER PUREE

Make the puree using the main recipe (page 67), omitting the apple, pear, and cinnamon and adding 2 pitted, peeled, and chopped peaches and ½ cup (120 ml) coconut milk (adjusting the water to 1 cup/240 ml). Cook, cool, and puree as instructed in the main recipe, adding ½ teaspoon freshly grated ginger to the blender.

 ### variation | OAT, RASPBERRY, STRAWBERRY, AND VANILLA PUREE

Make the puree using the main recipe (page 67), omitting the apple, pear, and cinnamon and adding 1 cup (125 g) raspberries (fresh or frozen) and 1 cup (150 g) trimmed and chopped strawberries (fresh or frozen). Cook, cool, and puree as instructed in the main recipe, adding ½ teaspoon vanilla extract to the blender.

LENTIL, CARROT, AND THYME PUREE, PAGE 66

Keep Avocado Green: If freezing the Oat, Avocado, and Spinach Puree, add a splash of lemon juice to help preserve the green avocado color.

OAT, AVOCADO, AND SPINACH PUREE, PAGE 68

CHICKEN PUREES

Prep Time 5 minutes
Cook Time 30 minutes
Yield about 12–20 oz (350–560 g)
Storage 3 days in fridge or
2 months in freezer

Chicken is full of protein, zinc, vitamin B6, and iron. Essential for healthy brain and organ development, it is important to incorporate iron-rich sources into your baby's diet at around six months of age, as babies' natural iron reserves start to dwindle at that time.

CHICKEN AND ORANGE PUREE *(shown opposite)*

There is nothing exciting about plain, pureed chicken, which is why I add some orange juice before roasting to give some zing and depth.

Ingredients:
- 1 boneless skinless chicken breast, cut in half horizontally
- ½ an orange, sliced
- 1 cup (240 ml) low- or no-sodium chicken broth, formula, or breastmilk

1 Preheat the oven to 400°F (200°C). Lay the chicken breast pieces out on a large sheet of aluminum foil, then top with the orange slices. Wrap the chicken in the foil to make a pouch with the seams facing up. Place it on a baking sheet. Bake for 30 minutes or until the chicken is cooked all the way through. Let cool to touch.
2 Transfer the chicken to a blender or food processor. Squeeze any remaining juices from the oranges into the blender and then discard. Add in ½ cup (120 ml) of broth and puree until smooth, adding additional liquid in ¼ cup (60 ml) increments if needed.

variation | CHICKEN, CARROT, POTATO, AND CUMIN PUREE

Make the puree using the main recipe (above)—orange slices are optional—adding 2 peeled and chopped carrots and 1 peeled and chopped small white potato to the foil pouch, sprinkling with 1 teaspoon ground cumin. Bake, cool, and puree as instructed in the main recipe.

variation | CHICKEN, PEA, BROCCOLI, AND CHIVE PUREE

Make the puree using the main recipe (above), omitting the orange and adding 1 cup (120 g) chopped broccoli and ½ cup (80 g) peas to the foil pouch. Bake, cool, and puree, adding ½ tablespoon chopped chives to the blender.

Also Good With: 1 cup (135 g) cooked brown rice added in—you can pulse a couple times for a chunky puree or completely puree for a smooth texture.

CHICKEN AND ORANGE PUREE, PAGE 70

variation | CHICKEN, PEACH, AND CILANTRO PUREE

Make the puree using the main recipe (page 70)—orange slices are optional—adding 2 pitted, peeled, and chopped peaches (fresh or frozen) to the foil pouch. Bake, cool, and puree as instructed in the main recipe, adding 1 tablespoon chopped fresh cilantro to the blender.

variation | CHICKEN, SWEET POTATO, TURNIP, AND SAGE PUREE

Make the puree using the main recipe (page 70)—orange slices are optional—adding ½ peeled and chopped sweet potato and ½ peeled and chopped turnip to the foil pouch. Bake, cool, and puree as instructed in the main recipe, adding 1 teaspoon chopped sage to the blender.

Also Good With: Add 1 cup (225 g) cooked farro to this puree.

BEEF PUREES

Prep Time 5 minutes
Cook Time 25 minutes
Yield about 12–20 oz (350–560 g)
Storage 3 days in fridge or
2 months in freezer

Full of iron, beef is a great puree to introduce early on in your baby's foodie adventures because maintaining a healthy level of iron is key for brain development. Beef puree is a natural way to replenish a baby's iron supply instead of using packaged fortified cereals.

BEEF AND OREGANO PUREE

Beef puree is usually a winner with babies. Month after month, readers pick this beef and oregano puree recipe as one of their top 10 favorite purees from my blog.

Ingredients:
- 8 oz (225 g) sirloin beef steak, cubed
- 2 cups (480 ml) low- or no-sodium beef broth or water
- 1 teaspoon dried oregano

1 Put the beef, broth, and oregano in a medium saucepan and bring to a boil over high heat. Turn to low and let simmer for 25 minutes or until the beef is cooked all the way through. Let cool slightly.
2 Use a slotted spoon to transfer the beef to a blender or food processor (reserving the broth), and puree until smooth, adding additional liquid in ¼ cup (60 ml) increments until you reach your desired consistency.

variation | BEEF, PUMPKIN, PEAR, AND SAGE PUREE

Make the puree using the main recipe (above), omitting the oregano, increasing the broth to 3 cups (720 ml), and adding 2 cups (240 g) chopped pumpkin (sweet potato also works well in this recipe), 2 cored and chopped pears, and ½ tablespoon chopped fresh sage. Cook, cool, and puree as instructed in the main recipe.

variation | MEXICAN BEEF, PINTO BEAN, RED BELL PEPPER, AND MILD CHILI PUREE

Make the puree using the main recipe (above), omitting the oregano, increasing the broth to 3 cups (720 ml), and adding 1 cup (240 g) cooked pinto beans, 1 cored and chopped red bell pepper, and 1 teaspoon mild chili powder. Cook, cool, and puree as instructed in the main recipe.

variation | BEEF, BROCCOLI, PEA, AND BALSAMIC VINEGAR PUREE *(shown below)*

Make the puree using the main recipe (page 72), omitting the oregano, increasing the broth to 3 cups (720 ml), and adding 1 cup (120 g) chopped broccoli, ½ cup (80 g) peas (fresh or frozen), and 1 teaspoon balsamic vinegar. Cook, cool, and puree as instructed in the main recipe.

BEEF, BROCCOLI, PEA, AND BALSAMIC VINEGAR PUREE, SEE ABOVE

SALMON PUREES

Prep Time 5 minutes
Cook Time 15 minutes
Yield about 12–20 oz (350–560 g)
Storage 3 days in fridge or
2 months in freezer

Salmon makes a super-power puree! Salmon (and any oily fish) is filled with omega-3 fatty acids, which aid brain, nerve, and eye development. I also find that because it is high in fat, salmon purees into a smooth and tasty puree for your baby.

SALMON AND LEMON ZEST PUREE *(shown opposite)*

This puree is great for introducing your baby to the nutritional goodness of salmon. Make sure that your little one has tried this simple puree before introducing salmon in any combination purees as fish can be an allergen for some babies.

Ingredients:

- 12 oz (350 g) salmon fillet, skin and bones removed and cut into 2 pieces
- 2 lemon slices
- ½ teaspoon grated lemon zest

1 Fill a medium saucepan with 2 inches (5 cm) of water and bring to a boil over high heat. Add the salmon to a steamer basket and cover with the lemon slices. Cover and steam for 10–15 minutes or until the salmon is cooked all the way through. Reserve the steamer water and let cool slightly.

2 Discard the lemon slices. Transfer the salmon and lemon zest to a blender or food processor, and puree until smooth, adding reserved steamer liquid in ¼ cup (60 ml) increments until you reach your desired consistency.

variation | SALMON, CARROT, LEMON, AND SHALLOT PUREE

Make the puree using the main recipe (above), but layer 2 peeled and chopped carrots in the steamer basket before topping with the salmon, increase the lemon to 2 slices on each piece of salmon, and sprinkle with 1 tablespoon chopped shallots. Cook, cool, and puree as in the main recipe, squeezing any remaining lemon juice from the slices into the blender (discard the lemon).

variation | SALMON, SPINACH, FENNEL, AND CLOVE PUREE

Make the puree using the main recipe (above)—lemon is optional— layering 1 trimmed and chopped fennel bulb in the steamer basket, followed by the salmon and 1 cup (30 g) packed spinach. Cook, cool, and puree as instructed in the main recipe, adding ¼ teaspoon ground cloves to the blender.

variation | SALMON, CORN, POTATO, AND CHILI POWDER PUREE

Make the puree using the main recipe (page 74)—lemon is optional—
layering 1 small peeled and chopped white potato in the steamer basket,
followed by the salmon and 1 cup corn (175 g), fresh or frozen. Cover and
steam for 15 minutes, then let cool and puree as instructed in the main
recipe, adding ½ teaspoon mild chili powder to the blender.

WHITE FISH AND TARRAGON PUREE, PAGE 76

Buy Wild Salmon: If
possible, purchase wild
salmon to maximize the
omega-3 content of your
baby's meals.

SALMON AND LEMON ZEST PUREE, PAGE 74

WHITE FISH PUREES

Prep Time 5 minutes
Cook Time 15 minutes
Yield about 12–20 oz (350–560 g)
Storage 3 days in fridge or
2 months in freezer

The first time I made a fish puree, my husband wasn't convinced. But it turns out that white fish is loaded with protein, omega-3 fatty acids, B vitamins, and selenium, which help aid cell growth and promote healthy thyroid function, so he quickly got on the fish-eating boat!

 ## WHITE FISH AND TARRAGON PUREE *(shown on page 75)*

After several tries, this recipe hit the mark. Creamy, mild, and versatile, this basic fish puree is able to mix into any combination you can dream up.

Ingredients:

- 1 teaspoon olive oil
- 1 medium fillet of white fish (such as tilapia, grouper, or sole)
- ½ teaspoon dried tarragon
- ½ cup (120 ml) water, low- or no-sodium vegetable or fish broth, formula, or breastmilk

1 Preheat the oven to 400°F (200°C). Line a medium baking dish with parchment paper and coat with ½ teaspoon olive oil. Place the fish in the baking dish, coat with the remaining oil, and sprinkle with tarragon. Bake for 10–15 minutes or until the fish is just cooked all the way through. Let cool slightly.

2 Transfer all the ingredients to a blender or food processor, and puree until smooth, adding additional liquid in ¼ cup (60 ml) increments if needed.

 ## variation | WHITE FISH, LEEK, AND ASPARAGUS PUREE

Make the puree using the main recipe (above)—tarragon is optional—layering the fish in a single layer along with 1 trimmed and chopped leek and 5 trimmed and chopped asparagus stalks, and drizzle with olive oil (you may need to increase olive oil by ½ teaspoon). Bake, cool, and puree as instructed in the main recipe.

Also Good With: There are so many herbs and spices that go with this puree combo—parsley, tarragon, lemon zest, garlic, dill, thyme, cumin, or even mint! Sprinkle one (or several) over the ingredients before baking, and try a new one each time.

variation | WHITE FISH, PEACH, CARROT, AND CUMIN PUREE

Make the puree using the main recipe (page 76), omitting the tarragon and adding 2 peeled and chopped carrots and 1 pitted and chopped peach to the baking dish in a single layer. Sprinkle with the olive oil and 1 teaspoon ground cumin. Bake for 10–15 minutes or until the fish and peaches are done, remove, then return the carrots to the oven for 30 minutes or until tender. Cool and puree as instructed in the main recipe.

Also Good With: For a well-rounded meal, try adding 1 cup (180 g) cooked quinoa to this puree for an extra dose of protein and fiber.

variation | WHITE FISH, ZUCCHINI, CILANTRO, AND GINGER PUREE

Make the puree using the main recipe (page 76), omitting the tarragon and adding 1 medium chopped zucchini to the baking dish. Bake, cool, and puree as instructed in the main recipe, adding ½ tablespoon chopped fresh cilantro and ½ teaspoon freshly minced ginger to the blender.

CLOSER LOOK
Omega-3 Fatty Acids

Including healthy omega-3 fatty acids in babies' and toddlers' diets helps to support brain development and both short- and long-term memory, and may reduce behavioral problems including anxiety, hyperactivity, and aggression. Wow! All of those amazing qualities come from adding just a couple of servings of salmon, flaxseeds, chia seeds, walnuts, or even spinach into your little one's weekly diet. For babies, try the Salmon, Spinach, Fennel, and Clove Puree (see page 74). For toddlers, check out the Mango, Oat, and Flaxseed Green Smoothie (see page 98). Yum.

FIRST FINGER FOODS

Your baby is now moving on to wanting to feed themselves, and you can almost hear them say "Let ME do it!" While finger foods need to be soft enough for baby to chew (or more likely gum), this doesn't mean that these foods have to be boring and bland. Seasoned with herbs and spices, the finger foods in this chapter are all winners in the taste department!

SIMMERED APPLES, CLOVES, AND GINGER

Prep time 5 minutes
Cook time 8–10 minutes
Yield ½ cup (150 g)
Storage 4 days in fridge or 3 months in freezer

Tender, sweet, and with a dash of spice, these apple pieces are great for your baby's first food. While some babies like their finger foods in long strips, others like theirs in small pea-size chunks—experiment and see what works best for your little one.

Ingredients:
- 1 eating apple, peeled, cored, and chopped
- ¼ teaspoon ground cloves
- ⅛ teaspoon ground ginger
- 3 tablespoons water

1 Put all the ingredients in a small saucepan and bring to a boil over medium heat.
2 Reduce heat to low and simmer for 8–10 minutes or until the apples are soft, stirring occasionally. Use a slotted spoon to transfer the apples to a paper towel and let completely cool.

Also Good With: I like to add a tiny sprinkle of ground cinnamon to the apple pieces before serving.

SIMMERED APPLES, CLOVES, AND GINGER, SEE ABOVE

PEACH AND CINNAMON

Prep Time 5 minutes
Cook Time 5 minutes
Yield 1 cup (225 g)
Storage 3 days in fridge

Unless your peach is extremely ripe, I find that they can be a little hard for babies to eat when they first start exploring finger foods. By gently simmering, the peaches intensify in flavor and are soft enough for your baby to enjoy.

 Ingredients:
- 1 peach (fresh or frozen), peeled, pitted, and chopped
- ¼ cup (60 ml) water
- ¼ teaspoon ground cinnamon

1 Put the peaches, water, and cinnamon in a medium saucepan and cook over medium heat for 5 minutes, stirring often.
2 Use a slotted spoon to transfer the peach chunks to a cutting board. Let cool, then chop the peaches into small chunks and serve.

PEACH AND CINNAMON, SEE ABOVE

COOKED VEGGIES

Prep time under 10 minutes, see recipes
Cook time varies, see recipes
Yield varies, see recipes
Storage varies, see recipes

Serve your baby all the colors of the rainbow with these bright, nutrient-dense cooked veggies. Feeding your baby a range of colorful produce ensures they receive all the essential nutrients needed for growth and development.

ROASTED ORANGEY SQUASH AND BEET *(shown on page 85)*

Soft and sweet, these roasted butternut squash and beets get a fun taste-twist (and vitamin C) from a splash of freshly squeezed orange juice.

Prep Time 10 minutes
Cook Time 20 minutes
Yield 2 cups (250 g)
Storage 4 days in fridge or 2 months in freezer

Ingredients:
- 2 cups (200–240 g) small cubed or finger-shaped butternut squash and beets (red or yellow work equally well—if using red beets, rinsing and drying them before roasting helps to stop their color spreading)
- 1 teaspoon olive oil
- 1 teaspoon freshly squeezed orange juice

1 Preheat the oven to 400°F (200°C) and line a baking sheet with aluminum foil, parchment paper, or a silicon mat. Toss the squash and beets with the olive oil and spread out on the baking sheet. Bake for 20 minutes, turning halfway through the cooking time, or until the beets are tender.
2 Let cool slightly, then drizzle with the orange juice. Toss gently and serve.

PUMPKIN AND CURRY

While I like the challenge of hacking apart an entire pumpkin, feel free to use an already cubed pumpkin in this recipe, halving the cooking time.

Prep Time 5–10 minutes
Cook Time 45–60 minutes
Yield 2 cups (250 g)
Storage 4 days in fridge or 3 months in freezer

Ingredients:
- ½ pie pumpkin, deseeded
- 2 teaspoons melted butter
- ½ teaspoon mild curry powder

1 Preheat the oven to 400°F (200°C). Place the pumpkin in a baking dish, skin side up, and add 1 inch (2.5 cm) of water. Bake for 45–60 minutes or until you can easily prick the skin of the pumpkin with a fork. Let cool slightly.
2 Scrape the pumpkin flesh from the skin and chop into pea-sized pieces. Toss with the melted butter and curry powder.

ASPARAGUS AND COCONUT OIL *(shown on page 85)*

Asparagus spears are naturally a great vegetable for babies to hold on to while they chew down on it. When tossed in a small amount of coconut oil, they help boost the immune system, ease digestion, and fight viruses.

Prep Time 5 minutes
Cook Time 10 minutes
Yield about 2 cups (400 g)
Storage 4 days in fridge or 3 months in freezer

Ingredients:
- 1 lb (450 g) asparagus, chopped, fresh or frozen
- ½ teaspoon coconut oil, melted

1 Pour about 2 inches (5 cm) of water into a medium saucepan and heat on medium until the water begins to boil. Place the asparagus in a steamer basket over the boiling water, and cover and cook for 8–10 minutes or until just tender. Remove with a slotted spoon and let cool slightly.
2 Chop the asparagus into pea-sized pieces and toss with ½ teaspoon melted coconut oil.

Also Good With: A pinch of lemon zest, ¼ teaspoon ground cumin, or ⅛ teaspoon ground cloves are some of my favorite spices to toss in with these asparagus bites.

CARROT AND CILANTRO

Carrots are full of beta-carotene and are the kings of promoting good eyesight. The best part is that these tender nuggets are sweet, delicious, and easy for your baby to devour. I like to pair these cooked carrots with chunks of ripe pear for a fun finger salad.

Prep Time 5 minutes
Cook Time 10 minutes
Yield 2 cups (400 g)
Storage 4 days in fridge or 3 months in freezer

Ingredients:
- 1 lb (450 g) carrots, peeled, trimmed, and chopped
- ½ teaspoon olive oil
- ½ teaspoon finely chopped cilantro

1 Pour about 2 inches (5 cm) of water into a medium saucepan and heat on medium until the water begins to boil. Place the carrots in a steamer basket over the boiling water. Cover and cook for 10 minutes or until just tender. Let cool slightly.
2 Chop the carrots into pea-sized pieces and toss with the olive oil and cilantro. Serve warm or cold.

ROASTED SWEET POTATOES AND PAPRIKA

Prep Time 5 minutes
Cook Time 30 minutes
Yield 1 cup (100 g)
Storage 4 days in fridge or
3 months in freezer

This recipe is great for a first finger food or as a toddler side dish. I love to mix up the spices and find that garlic powder, nutmeg, cinnamon, rosemary, thyme, or even cloves pair well with this recipe. *(shown opposite)*

 Ingredients:

- 1 small sweet potato, peeled and chopped into bite-size pieces, as shown opposite
- 1 teaspoon olive or melted coconut oil
- ½ teaspoon paprika

1 Preheat the oven to 375°F (190°C) and line a baking sheet with aluminum foil or a silicon mat. Place the sweet potatoes on the baking sheet, drizzle with the oil, and sprinkle with paprika. Mix well with your hands so that the potato is evenly coated.

2 Roast for 25–30 minutes in the oven or until the sweet potato pieces are tender, stirring halfway through baking time. Let cool slightly.

CLOSER LOOK
Should Your Baby Feed Herself?

Baby-led weaning is a popular method for feeding your baby. The basic theory is that you actually skip baby purees altogether and start feeding your baby finger foods from the very beginning.

In my experience, a baby seems to have a firm idea of what type of food they want to eat. My first daughter, Ellie, ate purees like they were going out of style—she couldn't get enough! With my second daughter, Parker, she liked purees just fine, but from the very beginning, she also wanted to feed herself with more solid food. So from day one of weaning, we provided her with a mix of purees and finger foods. It's important when feeding your baby to keep an open mind and try different options. Whether your little one prefers purees or solids, the most important thing you can do is to provide healthy, colorful, and nutritious food—how they eat this food is up to them. (For more information on Baby-led Weaning and feeding stages see pages 14–17.)

ASPARAGUS AND COCONUT OIL, PAGE 83

ROASTED SWEET POTATOES AND PAPRIKA, PAGE 84

ROASTED ORANGEY SQUASH AND BEET, PAGE 82

STEAMED GREEN BEANS WITH LEMON ZEST

Prep time 5 minutes
Cook time 5 minutes
Yield 1 cup (140 g)
Storage 4 days in fridge or
3 months in freezer

These crispy green beans are a perfect shape for your baby to hold on to while they eat. The key is to gently steam them, so that the green beans hold their texture and don't become too soft for your baby to handle. *(shown opposite)*

Ingredients:

- 1 cup (140 g) green beans, trimmed and chopped
- ¼ teaspoon olive oil
- ½ teaspoon grated lemon zest

1 Pour 2 inches (5 cm) of boiling water into a medium saucepan. Put the green beans in a steamer basket and place it over the boiling water. Cover and cook for 5 minutes or until still slightly crispy.
2 Remove the beans from the steamer basket and let cool slightly before tossing them with the olive oil and lemon zest.

ROASTED BEETS AND THYME

Prep Time 5 minutes
Cook Time 30 minutes
Yield 1 cup (130 g)
Storage 4 days in fridge or
3 months in freezer

When roasted, beets turn into sweet little chunks of goodness. I like to serve these beets with a side of cubed feta, sliced black olives, and the Simple Chicken and Oregano (see page 88), for a well-rounded (and extremely fancy) baby meal. *(shown opposite)*

Ingredients:

- 2 medium beets, peeled and chopped
- 1 teaspoon olive oil
- ½ teaspoon freshly chopped thyme

1 Preheat the oven to 400°F (200°C) and line a baking sheet with aluminum foil or a silicon mat. Place the beets on the baking sheet and toss in the oil and thyme.
2 Bake for 25–30 minutes or until tender. Let cool slightly.

Colorful Roasted Beets: I love to roast both red and yellow beets at the same time so my baby has two bright and fun colors of food to enjoy at a meal.

CLOSER LOOK
Freezing Finger Foods

Most cooked finger foods are great reheated from frozen. Freezing portions will save you time in the kitchen so you aren't cooking five different 1-tablespoon servings at a time. My go-to method is to place the cooked and cooled items in a small airtight container, plastic sandwich baggie, or ice cube tray and then freeze. Remove the amount you need and either microwave until warmed all the way through and then cool; place in a small serving dish and thaw in the fridge overnight; or gently warm in a small skillet. Always check the internal temperature of reheated food before serving.

ROASTED BEETS AND THYME, PAGE 86

STEAMED GREEN BEANS WITH LEMON ZEST, PAGE 86

SIMPLE CHICKEN AND OREGANO

Prep Time 5 minutes
Cook Time 40 minutes
Yield 1 cup (150 g)
Storage 4 days in fridge or
3 months in freezer

This easy chicken recipe is not just for the beginner finger food eater—I cut these into strips and serve as a main meal for my toddlers all the time. Feel free to season with whatever you have on hand, and serve with a fun dip (see page 129).

Ingredients:
- 1 boneless and skinless chicken breast
- 1 tablespoon olive oil
- ½ teaspoon dried oregano

1 Preheat the oven to 425°F (220°C). Place the chicken on a 10-inch (25-cm) square of aluminum foil, drizzle with the olive oil and oregano, and wrap up like a package, making sure to fully close the ends of the foil to seal everything in.
2 Place the foil package on a baking sheet and roast for 35–40 minutes or until the juices run clear and the chicken is completely cooked. Let cool slightly, then cut into cubes and serve.

EASY FISH RECIPES

Prep Time 5 minutes
Cook time varies, see recipes
Yield varies, see recipes
Storage varies, see recipes

Full of omega-3 fatty acids, protein, and vitamins, fish is great for your baby! Try to use sustainable white fish from the get-go, and make sure that you carefully remove all skin and bones from the fish before cooking.

WHITE FISH, GINGER, AND ORANGE

This finger food is cooked with a touch of orange juice and ginger for a well-rounded flavor.

Prep Time 5 minutes
Cook Time 10 minutes
Yield 1 cup (175 g)
Storage 3 days in fridge or 2 months in freezer

Ingredients:

- juice from ½ an orange
- ½ teaspoon finely minced ginger
- 6 oz (175 g) white fish fillet, skin and bones removed (cod, tilapia, grouper, or snapper)
- 1 tablespoon olive oil

1 Mix together the orange juice and ginger in a small bowl. Pat dry both sides of the fish.
2 Warm the olive oil in a skillet over medium-high heat. Place the fish in the skillet and cook for 2–3 minutes, flip the fillet, and cook for another 2–3 minutes or until the fish is cooked all the way through.
3 Right before the fish is done, drizzle the orange juice and ginger on top. Remove from heat and let cool slightly. Cut into bite-size pieces and serve.

SALMON, LIME, AND PARSLEY

The great thing is that this recipe will grow with your little one—add a fun dip (see page 129), serve with the Steamed Green Beans with Lemon Zest (see page 86), or make into a salmon burger.

Prep Time 5 minutes
Cook Time 20 minutes
Yield 1 cup (175 g)
Storage 4 days in fridge or 3 months in freezer

Ingredients:

- 6 oz (175 g) salmon fillet, skin and bones removed
- juice from ½ a lime
- ½ teaspoon finely chopped fresh parsley

1 Preheat the oven to 450°F (230°C) and line a baking sheet with aluminum foil, parchment paper, or a silicon mat. Place the salmon on the baking sheet and bake for 12–15 minutes or until cooked all the way through.
2 Let cool slightly, then cut into small pieces. Gently toss in the lime juice and parsley.

SEARED TOFU, GINGER, AND CURRY

Prep Time 5 minutes
Cook Time 10 minutes
Yield 1 cup (120 g)
Storage 4 days in fridge
(not suitable for freezing)

Tofu is a great source of protein and iron and is a nutritious addition to any baby's diet. When shopping for tofu, look for the sprouted variety as it is less processed, is easier to digest, and aids in the absorption of nutrients.

Ingredients:
- ½ 14 oz (400 g) package sprouted tofu, drained
- 2 teaspoons olive oil
- ½ teaspoon ground ginger
- 1 teaspoon mild curry powder

1 Cut the tofu into 1-inch (2.5-cm) slices and pat dry. Heat the oil in a skillet over medium-high heat until hot. Cook the tofu for 4–5 minutes or until golden brown, turn, and continue to cook for another 4–5 minutes. Remove from heat.
2 Sprinkle with the ground ginger and curry powder and let cool slightly. Cut into small cubes and serve.

FARRO WITH BASIL AND OLIVE OIL

Prep time 5 minutes
Cook time 30 minutes
Yield 1 cup (225 g)
Storage 4 days in fridge or
3 months in freezer

Farro is my favorite grain for babies because it is big enough for them to grab onto but soft enough to chew. This recipe is also great for a toddler side dish or even tossed with some cooked chicken and greens for an adult meal. *(shown opposite)*

Ingredients:
- 1½ cups (360 ml) water or low- or no-sodium vegetable broth
- ½ cup (90 g) farro
- ½ teaspoon olive oil
- 1 teaspoon chopped fresh basil

1 Put the water or broth in a medium saucepan and bring to a boil. Add the farro to the pan, cover, reduce heat to low, and simmer for 25–30 minutes or until chewy. Remove from heat and let sit for 5 minutes. Drain any excess liquid and cool slightly.
2 Add the olive oil and basil to the drained farro, toss, and serve.

Grains for Finger Foods:
I love bigger grains such as farro and barley for a first finger food because they are some of the biggest grains and are a bit easier for little ones to feed themselves. These bigger grains are best for older babies and toddlers as they may be a choking hazard for younger babies.

FARRO WITH BASIL AND OLIVE OIL, PAGE 90

CARROT FRITTERS WITH NUTMEG

Prep Time 5 minutes
Cook Time 15 minutes
Yield 6–10
Storage 4 days in fridge or
3 months in freezer

These carrot fritters are perfect for babies to practice holding on to bigger pieces of food. While a fancier finger food, these delicious fritters are still soft enough for babies to be able to gum. *(shown opposite)*

 Ingredients:
- 4 carrots, peeled and grated
- ½ onion, finely grated
- ½ cup (60 g) whole wheat flour
- 2 tablespoons chopped fresh chives
- ½ teaspoon sea salt
- ½ teaspoon garlic powder
- ¼ teaspoon ground nutmeg
- 2 eggs
- 2 tablespoons water
- 2 tablespoons olive oil

1 Combine the carrots, onion, flour, chives, salt, garlic, and nutmeg in a medium bowl. Mix in the eggs and 2 tablespoons of water and stir until well incorporated.

2 Heat the oil in a skillet over medium-low heat. Spoon the carrot mixture—in 2-tablespoon patties for babies or ¼-cup patties for older toddlers—into the pan and cook for 4–5 minutes or until golden brown. Flip and flatten with the back of the spatula, and cook for another 4–5 minutes. Remove from heat and let cool slightly.

CARROT FRITTERS WITH NUTMEG, PAGE 92

SWEET POTATO WAFFLES

Prep Time 15 minutes
Cook Time 20 minutes
Yield 12–24
Storage 4 days in fridge or
3 months in freezer

These waffles are filled with nutrient-rich sweet potatoes and are perfect for babies, toddlers, and the entire family! These healthy carbs are perfect for a family breakfast or as an afternoon treat for your little ones. *(shown opposite)*

 Ingredients:

- 1½ cups (185 g) whole wheat flour
- 1 cup (90 g) instant oats
- 3 teaspoons baking powder
- 1 teaspoon ground cinnamon
- ¼ teaspoon salt
- 2 eggs
- 1 cup (240 ml) unsweetened milk of choice
- ½ cup (105 g) plain whole-fat yogurt
- 3 tablespoons coconut oil, melted
- ⅓ cup (80 g) sweet potato puree or applesauce
- 2 tablespoons maple syrup
- cooking spray or olive oil for greasing the waffle maker

1 Whisk together the flour, oats, baking powder, cinnamon, and salt in a large bowl until combined.

2 Whisk in the eggs, milk, yogurt, coconut oil, sweet potato puree, and maple syrup until all the ingredients are combined. Let stand for 10 minutes while you preheat the waffle maker. If the batter becomes too thick, add 1 tablespoon of milk at a time to make it thinner.

3 Pour roughly 2 tablespoons of batter onto a lightly greased waffle maker for baby-sized waffles or ¼ cup (60 ml) batter for toddler-sized waffles. Shut the lid and cook according to your waffle maker's directions.

4 Carefully lift the waffle out with a fork. Leave the waffles to cool slightly before serving. The batter will make 12 toddler-sized or 24 baby-sized waffles.

Also Good With: For a fun toddler breakfast, try serving these waffles with some blueberries (chopped up for younger toddlers or whole for older children) and yogurt.

SWEET POTATO WAFFLES, PAGE 94

MOVING ON + FOUR YEARS

Designed for growing children, these recipes offer delicious snacks, meals, and treats that will help them build a life-long relationship with healthy food. I have flagged the recipes in this chapter as best suited for children over the age of four as some of the recipes include nuts, seeds, and larger chunks of fruit or vegetables, which may be a choking hazard for younger children. You can adapt these recipes for younger children by chopping the ingredients very finely or pureeing to a smoother consistency.

GREEN SMOOTHIES

Prep Time 5 minutes
Cook Time none
Yield 2 small toddler-sized servings
Storage Serve immediately

The best way to get a picky eater to try a new fruit or vegetable is in a smoothie. Not only are they fast and easy to make, but they are also delicious to drink. Filled with a big serving of leafy greens, they also get sweetness from apples, bananas, and a drizzle of honey.

APPLE AND SPINACH GREEN SMOOTHIE *(shown opposite)*
This green smoothie might get an initial NO from your kiddo, but once they taste it, they will be asking for seconds in a heartbeat!

Ingredients:
- 1 small eating apple, peeled, cored, and chopped
- 1 ripe fresh or frozen banana
- 1 cup (240 ml) unsweetened milk of choice
- 1 cup (30 g) packed spinach
- 1 tablespoon honey
- 1 teaspoon chia seeds
- 1 cup ice, optional, see note on page 99

1 Put all the ingredients in a blender in the order listed above and blend for 1 minute or until smooth. Pour and serve.

variation | PEAR, CUCUMBER, AND GREEN GRAPE SMOOTHIE
Make the smoothie using the main recipe (above), adding ½ chopped cucumber and 1 cup (150 g) green grapes, and replace the apple with 1 cored and chopped pear. Blend as instructed in the main recipe.

variation | AVOCADO, PINEAPPLE, AND COCONUT GREEN SMOOTHIE
Make the smoothie using the main recipe (above), adding ½ ripe avocado, 1 cup (130 g) pineapple, and 2 tablespoons shredded coconut flakes. You might need to increase your milk to 2 cups (480 ml). Blend as instructed in the main recipe.

variation | MANGO, OAT, AND FLAXSEED GREEN SMOOTHIE
Make the smoothie using the main recipe (above), omitting the apple and adding ½ cup (75 g) frozen mango chunks, ¼ cup (25 g) oats, and 1 teaspoon flaxseeds. Blend as instructed in the main recipe.

variation | KIWI, KALE, AND MINT GREEN SMOOTHIE

Make the smoothie using the main recipe (page 98), omitting the spinach and adding 2 peeled and chopped kiwi, ½ cup (35 g) packed chopped kale, and 5 fresh mint leaves. Blend as instructed in the main recipe.

Make It Drinkable: I find that toddlers have an easier time drinking thinner-consistency smoothies, but feel free to add ½–1 cup ice to the blender before you process for a thicker consistency.

APPLE AND SPINACH GREEN SMOOTHIE, PAGE 98

PINK SMOOTHIES

Prep Time 5 minutes
Cook Time none
Yield 2 large toddler-sized servings
Storage Serve immediately or
1 month in freezer

Kids won't be able to get enough of these bright-pink smoothies. These delicious drinks are packed with antioxidant-filled raspberries and strawberries, calcium-loaded beets, protein-rich Greek yogurt, vitamin C-filled carrots, and fibrous oats.

RASPBERRY AND BEET SMOOTHIE WITH YOGURT *(shown opposite)*

I like to serve this for school-day breakfasts on the go. All three smoothies go in our personal smoothie cups—we all stroll to school, enjoying some morning sunshine and a glass of pink deliciousness.

Ingredients:
- 2 cups (250 g) frozen raspberries
- 1 banana, fresh or frozen, peeled
- 1 small beet, peeled and chopped or grated
- 2 tablespoons honey
- ½ cup (105 ml) plain Greek yogurt
- 2 cups (480 ml) unsweetened milk of choice
- 1 cup ice, optional, see note on page 99

1 Put all the ingredients in a blender in the order listed above and blend for 1 minute or until smooth (see tip on page 99 about consistency). Pour and serve.

....

Also Good With: Add ½ teaspoon ground cinnamon before blending.

....

variation | CHERRY, CARROT, GINGER, AND OAT SMOOTHIE

Make the smoothie using the main recipe (above), omitting the beet and yogurt, reducing the raspberries to 1 cup (125 g), and adding 1 cup (200 g) frozen cherries, 1 peeled and chopped or grated carrot, ½-inch (1-cm) piece of peeled ginger, and ¼ cup (25 g) rolled oats. Blend as instructed in the main recipe.

variation | GRAPEFRUIT, STRAWBERRY, AND DATE SMOOTHIE

Make the smoothie using the main recipe (above), omitting the raspberries, beet, and honey and adding 2 cups (300 g) frozen strawberries, ½ peeled and chopped grapefruit, and 4 pitted dates. Blend as instructed in the main recipe.

variation | BEET, PEACH, AND MINT SMOOTHIE

Make the smoothie using the main recipe (page 100), reducing the raspberries to 1 cup (125 g) and adding 1 cup (225 g) frozen peaches and 3 mint leaves. Blend as instructed in the main recipe.

Freezing Smoothies: For a handy option, freeze your smoothie in portion-size containers. Don't fill right to the top as the smoothie will expand a bit while freezing. To drink, simply thaw in the fridge overnight or for a couple of hours until fully defrosted.

RASPBERRY AND BEET SMOOTHIE WITH YOGURT, PAGE 100

CLOSER LOOK
No Juicer?

It's easy to make pressed juice without a juicer. Put all the ingredients in a high-speed blender and puree until smooth, adding 1–2 tablespoons of water or lemon juice if needed. Place a fine-mesh strainer over a large bowl or juice container, and pour the contents of the blender into the strainer. Use a spatula to press the puree down until all of the juice is squeezed out.

ABC PRESSED JUICE WITH GINGER, PAGE 103

PRESSED JUICES

Prep Time 5 minutes
Cook Time none
Yield 2 small servings
Storage 1 day in fridge

Although not as good as eating the whole produce, pressed juice provides an instant boost of micronutrients for little ones. Even better, I can get my toddlers to drink just about any fruit or vegetable when it is in juice form, without the added sugar in most store-bought juices.

ABC PRESSED JUICE WITH GINGER *(shown opposite)*

My kids love juices because they always get to help pick out the produce, load up the machine, and press the "go" button. This recipe is a winning flavor combo.

Ingredients:
- 2 red beets, trimmed and roughly chopped
- 2 eating apples, cored and roughly chopped
- 2 carrots, trimmed and roughly chopped
- 2-inch (5-cm) piece of ginger, peeled

1 Process all the ingredients through a juicer according to your manufacturer's directions. Stir the juice and serve over ice.

variation | ORANGE, CARROT, AND MANGO JUICE

Make the juice using the main recipe (above), omitting the beets and adding 2 peeled oranges and 1 peeled and pitted mango. Juice as instructed in the main recipe.

Also Good With: 4 fresh mint leaves give a fresh flavor to this juice.

variation | APPLE, STRAWBERRY, BEET, AND LIME JUICE

Make the juice using the main recipe (above), omitting the carrots and increasing the apples to 3 and adding 1 heaping cup (160 g) hulled strawberries and ½ peeled lime. Juice as instructed in the main recipe.

Also Good With: Add 2 packed cups (60 g) spinach for an extra dose of iron for your toddler.

variation | GOLDEN BEET, CUCUMBER, AND PEAR JUICE

Make the juice using the main recipe (above), omitting the carrots, reducing the apples to 1, and switching the beets you use to golden beets. Add ½ chopped cucumber and 2 cored and chopped pears. Juice as instructed in the main recipe.

WHOLE WHEAT MUFFINS

Prep Time 10 minutes
Cook Time 15–20 minutes
Yield 12 regular size or 36 mini muffins
Storage 1 week in airtight container or 2 months in freezer

The following muffin recipes are easy to make, and there is one for each season, so you will never be at a loss of what to bake for your family for breakfast or a mid-morning snack.

WHOLE WHEAT BLUEBERRY AND LEMON MUFFINS *(shown opposite)*

This muffin recipe is bursting with whole wheat flour for extra fiber and a little fruit goodness, so you won't mind when your toddler asks for seconds or even thirds.

Ingredients:
- 1½ cups (185 g) whole wheat flour (or mixture of whole wheat and white flour)
- 1 teaspoon baking powder
- 1 teaspoon baking soda
- ½ teaspoon salt
- ½ cup (140 g) honey or maple syrup
- ½ cup (105 g) plain Greek yogurt
- 1 egg
- ½ cup (115 g) applesauce or apple puree
- ⅓ cup (80 ml) unsweetened milk of choice
- 1 cup (145 g) blueberries (fresh or frozen)
- 1 teaspoon grated lemon zest

1 Preheat the oven to 375°F (190°C) and spray, grease, or line a muffin pan (use either a regular 12-hole muffin pan or 36-hole mini muffin pan).
2 Mix the flour, baking powder, baking soda, and salt together in a large bowl. Add the honey, yogurt, egg, applesauce, and milk and stir until just incorporated. Gently fold in the blueberries and lemon zest until just combined.
3 Fill the muffin cups two-thirds full. Bake for 15 minutes for mini muffins or 20 minutes for regular muffins, or until a toothpick inserted into the center comes out clean. Let cool for 5 minutes. Serve and enjoy.

Extra Sweetness: This muffin recipe isn't that sweet, so if you prefer your muffins on the sweeter side, increase the honey or maple syrup to 1 cup (280 g).

WHOLE WHEAT BLUEBERRY AND LEMON MUFFINS, PAGE 104

variation | PUMPKIN AND CRANBERRY MUFFINS

Make the muffins using the main recipe (page 104), omitting the blueberries, lemon, and applesauce and decreasing the whole wheat flour to 1 cup (125 g). Add ½ cup (45 g) rolled oats, 1 cup (230 g) pumpkin puree, 1 teaspoon vanilla extract, and 2 teaspoons pumpkin pie spice. Incorporate all ingredients, then fold in ⅔ cup (80 g) chopped fresh or dried cranberries. Bake and cool as instructed in the main recipe.

variation | DARK CHOCOLATE AND ZUCCHINI MUFFINS

Make the muffins using the main recipe (page 104), omitting the blueberries and lemon and decreasing the whole wheat flour to 1 cup (125 g). Add ½ cup (60 g) cocoa powder, 1 teaspoon ground cinnamon, ½ teaspoon ground cloves, 2 teaspoons vanilla extract, 1 cup (120 g) shredded and pressed zucchini, and ½ cup (80 g) dark chocolate chips (optional). Mix, bake, and cool as instructed in the main recipe.

variation | APPLE AND CINNAMON MUFFINS

Make the muffins using the main recipe (page 104), omitting the blueberries and lemon and adding 2 shredded or chopped cored eating apples (peeling is optional), 2 teaspoons ground cinnamon, and 1 teaspoon vanilla extract. Mix, bake, and cool as instructed in the main recipe.

Shredding Fruit and Vegetables: To press the zucchini, layer a couple of paper towels on the counter and place the shredded zucchini on top, then layer another couple of paper towels on top. Press down to remove some of the moisture. If shredding the apples, make sure to press the excess juice out by sandwiching the shredded apples between a couple of layers of paper towels or a cloth towel and rolling or pressing for 30–45 seconds.

Also Good With: For a fun, crunchy oat topping, mix together 1 cup (90 g) rolled oats, 1 tablespoon whole wheat flour, ¼ cup (50 g) brown sugar or coconut sugar, 4 tablespoons cold butter cut into chunks, and 2 tablespoons honey in a small bowl until it makes a crumbly mixture. Sprinkle on top of the muffins and bake according to directions in the main recipe (page 104).

KID-FRIENDLY MUFFINS

Prep Time 5 minutes
Cook Time 25 minutes
Yield 12 regular muffins
Storage 4 days in fridge or 3 months in freezer

These muffins are amazing for three reasons: they are full of eggs, which provide complete protein, omega-3's, and vitamin D to develop your little one's eyes, bones, and brain; they are grain-free, refined sugar-free, dairy-free, and nut-free; and they are delicious.

KID-FRIENDLY ORANGE POPPY SEED MUFFINS

My girls love these muffins, and I love that I can serve them for breakfast, lunch, or a snack and know they are getting a healthy snack full of protein.

Ingredients:

- ½ cup (60 g) coconut flour
- ½ cup (60 g) arrowroot powder
- 2 tablespoons poppy seeds
- 1 teaspoon baking soda
- ¼ teaspoon salt
- 6 eggs
- ⅓ cup (80 ml) orange juice, freshly squeezed is preferred
- ⅓ cup (80 ml) pure maple syrup
- ¼ cup (55 g) coconut oil, melted
- 2 teaspoons grated orange zest

> **Special Ingredients:**
> The coconut flour and arrowroot powder cannot be replaced by any other ingredient. Even though they may seem exotic, most health-food stores will carry them in the baking aisle.

1 Preheat the oven to 350°F (180°C) and grease a 12-hole muffin pan with coconut oil or line with paper muffin cups.
2 Whisk together the coconut flour, arrowroot powder, poppy seeds, baking soda, and salt in a medium bowl.
3 In another medium bowl, whisk together the eggs, orange juice, maple syrup, coconut oil, and orange zest.
4 Pour the wet ingredients into the dry ingredients and mix together until combined. Let the batter sit for 2–3 minutes to thicken.
5 Spoon the batter into the muffin pan, filling each cup two-thirds full, then bake for 25 minutes or until the tops are golden brown and the muffins feel firm to the touch. Let the muffins cool for 15 minutes on a wire rack before serving.

variation | DOUBLE CHOCOLATE MUFFINS WITH CREAM CHEESE TOPPING *(shown opposite)*

Start with the main muffin recipe (page 107), omitting the arrowroot powder, poppy seeds, orange juice, and orange zest and adding 6 tablespoons cocoa powder to the dry ingredients and 1 teaspoon vanilla extract to the wet ingredients. Mix as instructed in the main recipe and fill the muffin cups two-thirds full. In a small bowl, whisk together ⅓ cup (75 g) room temperature cream cheese and 2 tablespoons maple syrup until well combined. Drop a spoonful of the cream cheese mixture on top of all of the muffins. Bake and cool as instructed in the main recipe.

variation | PUMPKIN AND PECAN MUFFINS

Start with the main muffin recipe (page 107), omitting the poppy seeds, orange juice, and orange zest and adding ½ teaspoon baking soda and 2 teaspoons pumpkin pie spice to the dry ingredients and ½ cup (115 g) pumpkin puree, 1 teaspoon vanilla extract, and 1 teaspoon apple cider vinegar to the wet ingredients. Mix the wet ingredients into the dry ingredients and gently fold in ½ cup (50 g) chopped pecans. Bake and cool as instructed in the main recipe.

CLOSER LOOK
Allergies and Food Intolerances

Allergies are actually quite rare in babies. There is, however, a difference between allergies and intolerances. Intolerances are when the body cannot break down or digest a particular food. Wheat, gluten, dairy, soy, and corn are the major foods in this category, but other foods can also cause digestive troubles, as an infant's digestive tract is immature for the first year of life. Eating solid foods is new to a baby's digestive system, so give your child some time to get the hang of it all. In most cases, your baby will grow out of these intolerances.

Allergies, on the other hand, can include a severe reaction that can happen seconds or minutes after the exposure. Common foods to look out for are peanuts, tree nuts, shellfish, wheat, milk, soy, and eggs. Be mindful that if any immediate family member has an allergy, your baby might have it as well, so it is best to speak to your health-care provider on how to add this food into your baby's diet before you try any recipes.

Dairy-free Chocolate: If you want to make a dairy-free Double Chocolate Muffin with Cream Cheese Topping, omit the cream cheese topping and mix ¼ cup (40 g) dairy-free dark chocolate chips into the batter at the very end.

DOUBLE CHOCOLATE MUFFINS WITH CREAM CHEESE TOPPING, PAGE 108

YUMMY PANCAKES

Prep Time 5 minutes
Cook Time 20 minutes
Yield 16–20 pancakes
Storage 4 days in fridge or
3 months in freezer

These flour-free pancakes are our family favorite. This recipe makes a big batch of pancakes, so store any extra in the fridge or freezer for those busy weekday mornings. Full of protein and fiber, these fluffy pancakes will be a hit with your whole family.

 ## SIMPLE OAT PANCAKES WITH CHERRY AND ALMOND SYRUP *(shown opposite)*

The first time that I made these pancakes, Ellie grabbed six at once, stacked them on her plate, and dug in! She was in pancake heaven.

Ingredients:
- 2 cups (180 g) rolled oats
- ¾ cup (180 ml) unsweetened milk of choice
- ½ cup (105 g) plain full-fat yogurt, plus extra for serving (optional)
- 1 large ripe banana
- 1 tablespoon honey
- 1 teaspoon ground cinnamon
- 1½ teaspoons baking powder
- 2 eggs
- cooking spray or coconut oil, for coating the skillet

For the syrup:
- 1 cup (200 g) fresh or frozen cherries, pitted
- 1 cup (280 ml) maple syrup
- 1 teaspoon almond extract

1 First, make the syrup. Bring the cherries and maple syrup to a boil in a small saucepan. Reduce heat and simmer for 10 minutes. Add the almond extract and simmer for another 3 minutes. Let cool slightly. You can serve this chunky or pulse in a blender for a smoother syrup.

2 Now, make the pancakes. Put the oats, milk, yogurt, banana, honey, cinnamon, and baking powder, in the order listed, in a blender or food processor, and blend until smooth. Add the eggs and pulse until just incorporated. Let the mixture sit for 5 minutes. If the mixture is too thick, add a tablespoon of milk and pulse again.

3 Heat a skillet over medium-low heat. Spray or add coconut oil and heat until warmed. Pour in the pancake batter, using roughly 2 tablespoons for baby-sized pancakes or ¼ cup (60 ml) for toddler-sized pancakes. Cook for 3–4 minutes or until bubbles appear on the surface, then flip and cook for another 3–4 minutes. Remove the pancakes and let cool slightly before serving. Repeat until all of your batter is used.

4 Serve the pancakes with a spoonful of the cherry syrup and a dollop of yogurt (optional).

SIMPLE OAT PANCAKES WITH CHERRY AND ALMOND SYRUP, PAGE 110

variation | OATMEAL, BLUEBERRY, AND LEMON PANCAKES

Make the pancakes using the main recipe (page 110), and stir in
1 cup (145 g) blueberries (if using frozen, thaw first) and 2 teaspoons
grated lemon zest to the batter right before cooking. Cook as
instructed in the main recipe.

 ### variation | CHOCOLATE AND STRAWBERRY PANCAKES

Make the pancakes using the main recipe (page 110), and stir in
¼ cup (30 g) cocoa powder to the batter while blending. Cook as
instructed in the main recipe. Meanwhile, toss 1 cup (150 g) hulled
and chopped strawberries with ½ teaspoon vanilla extract and
1 tablespoon maple syrup. Serve the chocolate pancakes with the
coated strawberries on top.

variation | ROASTED BANANA PANCAKES WITH COCONUT CREAM

Preheat the oven to 375°F (190°C). Place 2 peeled bananas that
have been cut lengthwise on a lined baking sheet and sprinkle with
ground cinnamon. Roast for 15–20 minutes or until just brown.
Add 1 of the roasted bananas to the basic recipe (page 110), and cook
as instructed in the main recipe. Chop the remaining banana into
chunks for serving. Meanwhile, in a medium bowl, blend together 1
cup (240 ml) chilled coconut cream (full-fat coconut milk works if you
drain the top liquid off), 1 tablespoon maple syrup, and ½ teaspoon
vanilla extract, and beat in a mixer on high speed for 5–8 minutes or
until fluffy. Serve the warm pancakes with a dollop of coconut cream
and chunks of roasted bananas on top.

Also Good With: For older toddlers, these pancakes are also great
with ¼ cup (25 g) finely chopped, roasted pecan pieces mixed into
the batter right before cooking and a couple sprinkled on top to give
a little extra crunch.

 ### variation | PEACH PANCAKES WITH CLOVES AND GINGER

Make the pancakes using the main recipe (page 110), and stir
in 1 cup (225 g) finely chopped peaches (if using frozen, thaw
first), ¼ teaspoon ground cloves, and ¼ teaspoon ground ginger into
the batter right before cooking. Cook as instructed in the main recipe.

SIMPLE GRANOLAS

Prep Time 5 minutes
Cook Time 45 minutes
Yield 5 cups (1.2 kg)
Storage 2 months in
airtight container

Crunchy granola is a favorite at my house, and I always have at least two variations on hand. Granola is filled with good-for-you cholesterol, fiber, protein, and a hint of sweetness. It's perfect for topping yogurt or oatmeal, or for snacking right out of the container.

APRICOT AND ALMOND GRANOLA *(shown on page 114)*

You can customize granola any way you want—add some extra nuts or have no nuts at all, add any dried fruit you have on hand, and even add dark chocolate, because why not?

Ingredients:
- 2 cups (180 g) rolled oats
- 2 cups (220 g) sliced or slivered almonds
- ¼ cup (25 g) flaxseeds
- ⅓ cup (80 ml) maple syrup
- ¼ cup (60 ml) olive oil
- ¼ cup (70 g) honey
- ½ teaspoon sea salt
- ½ teaspoon ground cinnamon
- 1 teaspoon almond extract
- 1 cup (150 g) dried apricots, chopped

1 Preheat the oven to 300°F (150°C) and spray a baking sheet with olive oil or line with baking parchment. Combine all the ingredients, except the dried apricots, in a large bowl and mix until well incorporated.

2 Pour the oat mixture out onto the baking sheet and spread until even. Bake for 45 minutes, stirring every 15 minutes. Remove from the oven and let cool for 10 minutes. Stir in the dried apricots and place in an airtight container.

Toddler-friendly Granola: Granola is a great way to encourage your kid's love of wholesome nuts, seeds, and fruit. When serving granola to toddlers, make sure that any nuts and seeds are finely sliced, and chop the dried fruit into small pieces.

APRICOT AND ALMOND GRANOLA, PAGE 113

variation | DARK CHOCOLATE AND COCONUT GRANOLA

Make the granola using the main recipe (page 113), omitting the apricots, and cook for 30 minutes. Add 1 cup (75 g) shredded coconut flakes and bake for another 10 minutes. Let cool completely, then add 1 cup (160 g) dark chocolate chips. Cool and store as instructed in the main recipe.

 ## variation | PUMPKIN SPICE AND PECAN GRANOLA

Make the granola using the main recipe (page 113), omitting the apricots and replacing the almonds with 1 cup (100 g) finely chopped pecans and ½ cup (70 g) pepitas (pumpkin seeds). Replace the almond extract with vanilla extract and add 2 teaspoons pumpkin pie spice. Bake, cool, and store as instructed in the main recipe.

Also Good With: I love adding 1 cup (120 g) dried cranberries.

variation | NUT-FREE GRANOLA WITH DRIED CHERRY AND VANILLA

Make the granola using the main recipe (page 113), omitting the almonds and apricots and increasing the oats to 3 cups (270 g). Replace the almond extract with 2 teaspoons vanilla extract, and add 1 whisked egg white, ¼ teaspoon ground cloves, and ¼ teaspoon ground nutmeg. Bake as instructed in the main recipe, adding 1 cup (140 g) chopped dried cherries after baking. Cool and store as instructed in the main recipe.

CLOSER LOOK
Nuts and Seeds

Nutritional superstars, nuts and seeds are great foods to include in your baby's and toddler's diet. Packed full of protein to support healthy growth, they also contain antioxidants, vitamins, minerals, and omega-3 fatty acids. They're the perfect foods for an energetic little one.

Whole nuts and seeds are not suitable for first finger foods for your baby because of their potential as a choking hazard. However, you can easily add seeds blended into your baby's puree—for example, the Quinoa, Blueberry, Cherry, and Flaxseed Puree (see page 63). You can also include the nutritional goodness in your toddler's diet by making a delicious nut or seed butter (see page 135), adding some finely chopped nuts to oatmeal, or even tossing them into a healthy smoothie.

TASTY OATMEAL

Prep Time 5 minutes
Cook Time 5–15 minutes
Yield 3 toddler servings
(or 2 adult servings)
Storage 5 days in fridge

Oats are filled with two types of fiber, iron, and protein, which helps reduce the symptoms of asthma, guards against cancer, and boosts the body's immune system. A bowl of oatmeal will keep your little one healthy, happy, and full.

 BEET AND CARROT OATMEAL *(shown opposite)*
Shredded beets and carrots will make your oatmeal taste like carrot cake but will be packed with two servings of vegetables. You are guaranteed a nutritional win at any meal!

Ingredients:
- 2 cups (480 ml) water or unsweetened milk of choice
- 1 cup (90 g) rolled oats
- ½ red beet, peeled and shredded
- 1 carrot, peeled and shredded
- 1 teaspoon ground cinnamon
- ¼ teaspoon ground cloves
- ⅛ teaspoon ground nutmeg
- 2 tablespoons raisins

1 Bring the water or milk to a boil in a saucepan over medium heat. Add all the ingredients except the raisins, stir, and bring back to a boil. Turn the heat down to low and simmer for 10 minutes or until all the water or milk is evaporated, stirring occasionally. Let cool slightly.

2 Spoon into bowls and add the raisins along with any extra toppings you desire—cream, chopped nuts, maple syrup, honey, flaxseeds, or a sprinkle of cinnamon.

Younger Baby Tip: This oatmeal is amazing when pureed and served to your baby for a fun and spiced-up oatmeal breakfast.

BEET AND CARROT OATMEAL, PAGE 116

variation | STRAWBERRY, VANILLA, AND CHIA SEED OATMEAL

Make the oatmeal using the main recipe (page 116), cooking just the oats and water to start with as instructed. Meanwhile, in a small saucepan, bring 2 cups (300 g) hulled strawberries and 2 tablespoons of water to a simmer for 5–10 minutes or until the strawberries are soft. Transfer the strawberries and their juices to a blender or food processor, and add 2 tablespoons honey, 1 teaspoon vanilla extract, and 1 teaspoon chia seeds, then puree until smooth. In bowls, layer the strawberry puree and oatmeal in alternating layers. Drizzle with cream and serve.

variation | TOASTED COCONUT AND FLAXSEED OATMEAL

Make the oatmeal using the main recipe (page 116), cooking the oats and water as instructed and adding 1 teaspoon ground cinnamon. Meanwhile, in a small skillet, heat ½ cup (35 g) shredded coconut and 1 tablespoon flaxseeds over medium heat for 5 minutes or until golden brown, stirring often. Spoon the oatmeal into bowls and sprinkle with the coconut and flaxseeds.

variation | CHERRY, PISTACHIO, AND CACAO NIB OATMEAL

Make the oatmeal using the main recipe (page 116), cooking the oats and water as instructed and adding 1 teaspoon ground cinnamon and ½ cup (100 g) pitted and roughly chopped fresh or frozen cherries. Meanwhile, in a small skillet, heat 2 tablespoons chopped pistachios over medium heat for 5 minutes or until toasted, stirring often. Spoon the oatmeal into bowls and, for older toddlers, sprinkle with pistachios and some cacao nibs.

FRUIT BARS

Prep Time 5 minutes
Cook Time 1 hour
Yield 24 toddler bites
Storage 7 days in an airtight container in fridge

My girls love the sweet, salty, and chewy taste of these bars, and I love that they are filled with wholesome nuts and fruit that pack in essential vitamins and protein.

 ## CHERRY AND CHOCOLATE FRUIT BARS *(shown on pages 120–121, 122)*
Cherries and chocolate are taste companions. While I use pecans in this version, feel free to swap them out for almonds if you prefer.

Ingredients:
- 1 cup (100 g) pecans
- 1 cup (140 g) dried cherries, halved
- ½ cup (65 g) dates, pitted
- ¼ cup (30 g) cocoa powder
- ⅛ teaspoon salt
- 1 tablespoon coconut oil, melted
- ⅓ cup (55 g) dark chocolate chips or pieces

1 Line an 8 x 8 inch (20 x 20 cm) baking dish with parchment paper or plastic wrap and set aside.
2 Put the pecans in a food processor and pulse until they are roughly chopped. Add half the cherries, the dates, cocoa powder, and salt to the food processor and pulse until roughly combined.
3 Add the coconut oil and continue to pulse until all the ingredients are combined and the mixture starts sticking together.
4 Add the remaining dried cherries and the chocolate chips and pulse 10–15 times or until the cherries and chocolate chips are broken down yet still chunky.
5 Transfer the nut mixture to the prepared baking dish and press down evenly and firmly with a spatula. Make sure to press the mixture tightly into the corners.
6 Transfer to the fridge and let sit for 1 hour. Cut into bars or bites and serve.

Dried Fruit Tip: If your dried fruit is hard, soak it in hot water for 5–10 minutes and then pat it dry before using.

LEMON, BLUEBERRY, AND CHIA SEED FRUIT BARS, PAGE 122

CHERRY AND CHOCOLATE FRUIT BARS, PAGE 119

variation | LEMON, BLUEBERRY, AND CHIA SEED FRUIT BARS *(shown on pages 120–121 and below)*

Use 1 cup (170 g) cashews, 1 cup (135 g) pitted dates, ⅛ teaspoon salt, 1 tablespoon melted coconut oil, 2 tablespoons lemon juice, and 2 teaspoons grated lemon zest, and mix as instructed in the main recipe (page 119). Add ½ cup (60 g) dried blueberries and 1 tablespoon chia seeds, and pulse until the blueberries are incorporated but still chunky. Continue as instructed in the main recipe.

variation | PB & J NUT BARS

Use ¾ cup (125 g) roasted peanuts, 1 cup (135 g) pitted dates, ⅛ teaspoon salt, and 1 tablespoon melted coconut oil, and mix as instructed in the main recipe (page 119). Add ¼ cup (50 g) roasted peanuts and ¼ cup (35 g) packed dried cherries, and pulse until just incorporated but still chunky. Continue as instructed in the main recipe.

variation | DOUBLE CHOCOLATE AND MINT FRUIT BARS

Use 1 cup (100 g) walnuts, 1¼ cups (170 g) pitted dates, ⅛ teaspoon salt, 1 tablespoon melted coconut oil, 6 tablespoons cocoa powder, 3–5 drops peppermint extract, and ⅓ cup (55 g) dark chocolate chips. Follow the instructions in the main recipe (page 119).

CHERRY AND CHOCOLATE FRUIT BARS, PAGE 119 AND LEMON, BLUEBERRY, AND CHIA SEED FRUIT BARS, SEE ABOVE

FINGER SALADS

Prep Time 5 minutes
Cook Time none
Yield about 1–1½ cups (100–150 g)
Storage 3 days in fridge

Finger salads are a fun way for little fingers to eat a variety of flavors, textures, and produce in a single serving. I make these salads for the kiddos who are just starting out eating solid food, but they are good enough for anyone to eat, including you!

 ## BLACKBERRY, HONEYDEW, AND ORANGE FINGER SALAD *(shown on page 124)*

This colorful fruit-filled finger salad is a great mix of tastes—sweet, tangy, and citrusy. I love to serve this to my toddler and then toss some along with a little cooked chicken onto a bed of lettuce for a healthy lunch for myself.

Ingredients:
- ½ cup (70 g) blackberries, halved
- ½ cup (80 g) honeydew melon, balled or cut into dime-sized pieces
- ½ an orange, peeled and chopped
- juice from ½ an orange

1 Put all the ingredients in a small bowl and gently mix. Serve immediately.

CLOSER LOOK
Organic Produce

Organic produce is any produce grown in its natural state without the use of synthetic chemicals, and it cannot include genetically modified organisms (GMO). Full of nutritional goodness, it is recommended to use organic produce for your kids' food. Here are my top tips to lessen the organic grocery bill:

- Look for organic produce that is in season and therefore cheaper.

- Look in the frozen food aisle. Organic produce will have been picked and flash frozen at the height of freshness.

- Start your own garden. As intimidating as that is, I am sure you won't kill your basil as fast as I can. Plus, kids will love helping out.

- Join a local Community Supported Agriculture (CSA) or community garden. Many CSA farms offer discounts on subscription if you volunteer your time.

KALE, APPLE, PUMPKIN SEED, AND OLIVE OIL FINGER SALAD, PAGE 125

BLACKBERRY, HONEYDEW, AND ORANGE FINGER SALAD, PAGE 123

variation | KALE, APPLE, PUMPKIN SEED, AND OLIVE OIL FINGER SALAD *(shown opposite)*

Toss together ½ cup (35 g) finely chopped and destemmed kale; ½ peeled, cored, and chopped eating apple; 1 tablespoon toasted pumpkin seeds; and 1 tablespoon olive oil until all the ingredients are mixed. Refrigerate for 30 minutes or long enough for the olive oil to soften the kale, then serve.

 variation | GOLDEN BEET, GRAPEFRUIT, AND EDAMAME FINGER SALAD

Toss together 1 cooked, peeled, and chopped golden beet; ¼ peeled and chopped grapefruit; and 2 tablespoons cooked edamame until all the ingredients are well mixed. If the grapefruit is a little too sour for your little one, try adding a splash of freshly pressed apple juice or a squeeze of orange juice.

 variation | GREEN GRAPE, CUCUMBER, STRAWBERRY, AND LIME FINGER SALAD

Toss together ½ cup (75 g) halved or quartered green grapes; ½ cup (105 g) peeled, deseeded, and chopped cucumber; ½ cup (75 g) hulled and chopped strawberries; and ½ squeezed lime until all the ingredients are well mixed.

 variation | RED PEPPER, WHITE BEAN, PEAR, AND CILANTRO FINGER SALAD

Toss together ½ cup (70 g) chopped red bell pepper; ½ cup (70 g) cooked, washed, and drained white beans (you can cut these in half if they are too large); ½ peeled, cored, and chopped pear; and ½ teaspoon chopped fresh cilantro until all the ingredients are well mixed. (See tip below for advice on storage.)

> **Storage Tip for Pears and Apples:**
> If storing a salad containing pears or apples for longer than a day, mix a splash of lemon or lime juice into the salad so the pears or apples don't brown.

FRUIT DIPS

Prep Time 5 minutes
Cook Time none
Yield 1 cup (220 g);
4 toddler servings
Storage 4 days in fridge

Sometimes you just need a little something-something to up your kiddo's fruit game. These dips are made for such occasions. Full of protein-rich yogurt and a ton of fun flavors, these dips will surprise your toddler with a fun way for them to eat more fruit.

 ### CREAMY CINNAMON AND VANILLA FRUIT DIP *(shown opposite)*

I am not even going to lie—I mix this together right in the yogurt container. The girls cannot get enough!

Ingredients:
- 1 cup (215 g) plain yogurt (see Yogurt Tip below)
- 2 tablespoons honey
- 1 teaspoon vanilla extract
- ½ teaspoon ground cinnamon

1 Stir all the ingredients together in a small bowl or yogurt container until well combined. Serve and enjoy.

Yogurt Tip: You can use either Greek or standard yogurt in this recipe. I find that Greek yogurt makes a thicker dip and is better for the little ones who are just starting to dip (the Greek yogurt won't make as big a mess). However, my older toddler prefers the standard yogurt for her dips. Use either or a mixture of both.

CREAMY CINNAMON AND VANILLA FRUIT DIP, PAGE 126

variation | PUMPKIN PIE SPICE FRUIT DIP

Mix together ¾ cup (155 g) plain yogurt, ¼ cup (60 g) pumpkin puree, 2 tablespoons honey, 1 teaspoon pumpkin pie spice, and ½ teaspoon vanilla extract in a small bowl. Serve and enjoy.

variation | AVOCADO AND CHOCOLATE FRUIT DIP

Mix together ½ cup (105 g) plain yogurt, ½ ripe avocado, 3 tablespoons cocoa powder, 3 tablespoons honey, ½ teaspoon vanilla extract, and ¼ teaspoon sea salt in a small bowl or food processor. Serve and enjoy.

variation | HONEY AND LIME FRUIT DIP

Mix together 1 cup (215 g) plain yogurt, 2 tablespoons honey, 1 tablespoon lime juice, and ½ teaspoon lime zest in a small bowl. Serve and enjoy.

CREAMY CINNAMON AND VANILLA FRUIT DIP, PAGE 126

SAVORY DIPS

Prep Time 5 minutes
Cook Time none
Yield about ¾ cup (165 g)
Storage 4 days in fridge

It can be hard to get your kids to eat their veggies—so when the little ones are turning their heads away, whip up one of these easy veggie dips. Made with yogurt and pantry ingredients, these dips will quickly become your kids' favorite part of meal time.

LEMON AND GARLIC DIP *(shown on page 130)*

This tasty dip is easy to make in a flash and will be quickly devoured because dips of any kind are universally cherished by all kids.

Ingredients:
- 1 cup (215 g) plain yogurt (see Dairy-Free Advice below)
- 1 garlic clove, minced
- 1 tablespoon lemon juice
- ½ teaspoon grated lemon zest
- 2 tablespoons chopped fresh chives
- salt and pepper, to taste

1 Mix all the ingredients together in a small bowl or food processor. Serve and enjoy.

Dairy-Free Advice:
You can substitute full-fat coconut milk or cream for the yogurt in any of these recipes to create a dairy-free version. However, keep in mind that coconut milk lacks the protein content of dairy yogurt.

What to Dip: These dips aren't just for veggies. They are great served with sliced pita bread (as shown), chicken or fish sticks, or spread onto grilled cheese sandwiches.

LEMON AND GARLIC DIP, PAGE 129

MANGO AND CILANTRO DIP, PAGE 131

variation | CURRY, HONEY, AND MUSTARD DIP

Mix together ½ cup (105 g) plain yogurt, 3 tablespoons honey, 3 tablespoons yellow or grain mustard, 1 teaspoon mild curry powder, and ¼ teaspoon salt in a small bowl. Serve and enjoy.

variation | THAI PEANUT AND GINGER DIP

Mix together ½ cup (105 g) plain yogurt, ⅓ cup (85 g) peanut butter, 2 tablespoons honey, 1 teaspoon minced ginger, 1 tablespoon soy sauce, and 1 tablespoon lemon juice in a small bowl. Serve and enjoy.

variation | MANGO AND CILANTRO DIP *(shown opposite)*

Blend together 1 pitted and peeled mango, ½ cup (105 g) plain yogurt, 2 tablespoons honey, 1 tablespoon lime juice, 2 tablespoons chopped cilantro, ½ teaspoon ground cumin, and ¼ teaspoon salt in a blender or food processor. Serve and enjoy.

BALLS OF ENERGY

Prep Time 5 minutes
Cook Time 1 hour
Yield 20
Storage 1 week in fridge

Energy balls are the perfect on-the-go healthy snack for little hands. Full of whole foods such as fiber-rich oats and protein-packed nuts, these balls will give your little one a burst of energy. Kids can have fun helping make these simple snacks with you.

 ## CASHEW, HONEY, AND SESAME BALLS OF ENERGY *(shown opposite)*
Whenever I start making these, Ellie pulls her stool over to the counter, helps roll some of the dough into a little ball, pops it right into her mouth, and heads off to her next adventure!

Ingredients:
- 1 cup (90 g) rolled oats
- ½ cup (120 g) Cashew and Cinnamon Butter (see page 136)
- ½ cup (85 g) cashews, finely chopped
- ⅓ cup (45 g) white sesame seeds
- ⅓ cup (95 g) honey
- 1 teaspoon vanilla extract

1 Combine all the ingredients in a bowl until thoroughly mixed. Cover and chill in the fridge for 30 minutes—this will make the mixture easier to roll.
2 Roll small amounts of mixture into 20 1-inch (2.5-cm) balls and place in an airtight container. Return to the fridge to chill for another 30 minutes. Serve and enjoy.

> **Get Ahead Tip:** These are great snacks to have on hand for when your toddler needs a quick energy boost. Make a batch and store them in an airtight container in the fridge to have ready to go throughout the week.

CASHEW, HONEY, AND SESAME BALLS OF ENERGY, PAGE 132

TOASTED COCONUT AND DARK CHOCOLATE BALLS OF ENERGY, PAGE 134

variation | ALMOND AND DRIED BLUEBERRY BALLS OF ENERGY

Combine 1 cup (90 g) rolled oats, ½ cup (120 g) Roasted Almond and Vanilla Butter (see page 135), ½ cup (60 g) dried blueberries, ½ cup (140 g) honey, ⅓ cup (30 g) ground flaxseeds, ¼ cup (40 g) finely chopped almonds, and 1 teaspoon vanilla extract in a bowl. Mix thoroughly and chill for 30 minutes. Continue as instructed in the main recipe (page 132).

variation | OATMEAL AND RAISIN BALLS OF ENERGY

Combine 1 cup (90 g) rolled oats, ½ cup (120 g) almond or peanut butter, ½ cup (80 g) raisins, ⅓ cup (90 g) honey, ¼ cup (25 g) finely chopped walnuts, ½ teaspoon ground cinnamon, and 1 teaspoon vanilla extract in a bowl. Mix thoroughly and chill for 30 minutes. Continue as instructed in the main recipe (page 132).

variation | TOASTED COCONUT AND DARK CHOCOLATE BALLS OF ENERGY *(shown on page 133)*

Combine 1 cup (90 g) rolled oats, ½ cup (120 g) almond or peanut butter, ½ cup (35 g) toasted shredded coconut, ⅓ cup (55 g) dark chocolate chips, and 1 teaspoon vanilla extract in a bowl. Mix thoroughly and chill for 30 minutes. Continue as instructed in the main recipe (page 132).

CASHEW, HONEY, AND SESAME BALLS OF ENERGY, PAGE 132

TOASTED COCONUT AND DARK CHOCOLATE BALLS OF ENERGY, PAGE 134

NUT BUTTERS

Prep Time 15 minutes
Cook Time 7–9 minutes
Yield 2 cups (480 g)
Storage 1 month in airtight container in the fridge or pantry

Want to keep your toddler entertained for 20 minutes? Make some nut butter with them! They can help pour the nuts into the food processor, flip the switch to start, and finally they can sit and stare at the machine as it grinds the nuts into a creamy, smooth butter.

 ROASTED ALMOND AND VANILLA BUTTER *(shown on page 137)*

The real treat comes when it's all done and you get to spoon-feed each other the amazing nut butter you just made together straight from the bowl.

Ingredients:
- 2 cups (340 g) raw almonds
- 2 teaspoons maple syrup
- 1 tablespoon coconut oil
- ¼ teaspoon sea salt
- 2 teaspoons vanilla extract

1 Put the almonds in a large skillet over medium heat and roast for 7–9 minutes or until brown and toasted, stirring frequently. Let cool slightly.
2 Transfer the almonds to a blender or food processor, and pulse a couple times. Let the machine run for 5 minutes, scraping down the sides as needed.
3 Add the remaining ingredients and blend for another 5–10 minutes or until the nut butter is smooth and shiny, scraping down the sides as needed. Transfer to an airtight container to store.

Nut Butters for Younger Children:
Creamy, smooth nut and seed butters are a good way to introduce the nutritional goodness of nuts and seeds into a younger child's diet. Nuts and seeds should be fully processed into a smooth consistency before serving to younger children to avoid any risk of choking. Speak to your pediatrician if you have any concerns about introducing nuts or seeds to your child.

variation | ROASTED PEANUT AND HONEY BUTTER

Begin by roasting 2 cups (340 g) raw, unsalted peanuts as instructed in the main recipe (page 135) for 5–7 minutes. Let cool slightly. Transfer to a blender or food processor, and blend for 3 minutes, scraping down the sides as needed. Add 1 tablespoon coconut oil, 2 tablespoons honey, ¼ teaspoon ground nutmeg, and ¼ teaspoon salt, and blend for another 3 minutes or until the nut butter is smooth and shiny.

 ### variation | HAZELNUT AND CHOCOLATE BUTTER

Begin by roasting and blending 2 cups (260 g) hazelnuts as instructed in the main recipe (page 135). Add 4 tablespoons cocoa powder, 2 tablespoons coconut oil, 1 teaspoon vanilla extract, ½ teaspoon ground cinnamon, and ¼ teaspoon salt, and blend for another 5 minutes or until the nut butter is smooth and shiny.

 ### variation | CASHEW AND CINNAMON BUTTER

Begin by roasting and blending 2 cups (340 g) cashew pieces as instructed in the main recipe (page 135). Add 1 tablespoon coconut oil, 2 tablespoons honey, 1 teaspoon ground cinnamon, and ¼ teaspoon salt, and process for another 5 minutes or until the nut butter is smooth and shiny.

 ### variation | SUNFLOWER SEED, MAPLE SYRUP, AND CLOVE BUTTER

Begin by roasting 2 cups (280 g) raw sunflower seeds as instructed in the main recipe (page 135) for 5–7 minutes, then let cool. Transfer to a blender or food processor, and blend for 5 minutes, scraping down the sides as needed. Add 2 tablespoons coconut oil, 1 tablespoon maple syrup, 1 teaspoon ground cinnamon, ½ teaspoon ground cloves, and ¼ teaspoon sea salt, and process for another 5 minutes or until the nut butter is smooth and shiny.

Buying Nuts: Since you are going to be blending the nuts, you can always buy them in pieces rather than in the whole form to save yourself some money.

ROASTED ALMOND AND VANILLA BUTTER, PAGE 135

BAKED VEGETABLE CRUNCHERS

Prep Time 15 minutes
Cook Time 20–30 minutes
Yield 4–6 toddler servings
Storage Best served the same day, but can be stored at room temperature for 3 days

These baked vegetable crunchers are a great addition to any toddler lunch, a fun after-school snack, or a dish for a kid's party. Full of fiber, vitamin C, beta-carotene, and powerful antioxidants, you won't mind when the entire batch is wiped out in five minutes.

  ### CINNAMON SWEET POTATO CRUNCHERS *(shown on page 140)*
Cinnamon is a perfect partner for these sweet potato crunchers! For a fun flavor contrast, I love to pair with the Lemon and Garlic Dip (see page 129) or the Super Simple Hummus (see page 139).

Ingredients:
- 2 sweet potatoes
- 1 tablespoon olive oil
- ½ teaspoon sea salt
- ½ teaspoon ground cinnamon

1 Preheat the oven to 375°F (190°C). Place wire racks on top of two baking sheets. Slice the sweet potatoes into ⅛-inch (3-mm) slices, or as thin as possible, with a mandolin or a sharp knife, making sure the slices are uniform for even baking. Lay the slices in individual layers on paper towels and press until dry.
2 In a large bowl, lightly toss the slices with the olive oil. Sprinkle with the salt and cinnamon, and toss until well coated.
3 Lay the slices in a flat layer on the wire rack and bake for 20–30 minutes or until golden brown, rotating the trays halfway through the baking time. Check the slices periodically during cooking to remove any chips that are done early. I find that the slices do not cook all at the same time; some take 20 minutes, while others take 30 minutes.
4 Remove from oven and let cool on a wire rack for 10 minutes. Serve and enjoy.

 ### variation | ROOT VEGETABLE CRUNCHERS WITH ROSEMARY
Follow the directions using the main recipe (above), but use 2 golden beets, 3 carrots, and 2 parsnips in place of the sweet potatoes; 1 tablespoon olive oil; ½ teaspoon sea salt; and 1 tablespoon crushed rosemary. Bake for 20 minutes or until golden brown, rotating the trays halfway through. The parsnips tend to bake faster, so make sure to watch them for the last 5 minutes of the baking time.

HUMMUS

Prep Time 5 minutes
Cook Time none
Yield 8 toddler servings
Storage 1 week in fridge

I'm a bit obsessed with making my own hummus, and these five recipes are my household favorites. Full of fiber, iron, and protein-rich beans, hummus helps digestive health, eyesight, and the development of muscles and internal organs.

SUPER SIMPLE HUMMUS *(shown on page 140)*

When Parker was a baby, she couldn't get enough of this Super Simple Hummus being spoon-fed to her. Now she digs in with crackers, cut veggies, or even just her fingers!

Ingredients:
- 15 oz (425 g) can chickpeas, drained, liquid reserved
- 2 tablespoons olive oil
- 2 tablespoons lemon juice
- 1 garlic clove
- 1 teaspoon ground cumin
- salt to taste (optional)

1 Put all the ingredients in a blender or food processor, and blend until smooth, adding the reserved chickpea water 1 tablespoon at a time if needed. Serve and enjoy.

Tahini Tip: I have left the tahini out of this recipe because I know many schools are going nut- and seed-free these days. If you want to add it in for older toddlers, be my guest. I would recommend using 2 tablespoons for the Super Simple Hummus recipe.

CINNAMON SWEET POTATO CRUNCHERS, SERVED WITH SUPER SIMPLE HUMMUS, PAGES 138 AND 139

variation | ROASTED GARLIC AND ROSEMARY HUMMUS

Make the hummus using the main recipe (page 139), adding 1 head of roasted garlic (see Garlic Tip below) and 1 tablespoon fresh chopped rosemary leaves. Blend until smooth.

variation | GREEN CHILI AND LIME HUMMUS

Make the hummus using the main recipe (page 139), adding 2 tablespoons chopped mild green chilies and 1 tablespoon peanut butter (optional), and substitute lime juice for the lemon juice. Blend until smooth.

variation | SUN-DRIED TOMATO AND BASIL HUMMUS

Make the hummus using the main recipe (page 139), adding ⅓ cup (35 g) drained sun-dried tomatoes in olive oil, 2 tablespoons of olive oil from the jar, 2 tablespoons chopped fresh basil, and ⅛ teaspoon pepper. Blend until smooth.

variation | PINEAPPLE AND MINT HUMMUS

Make the hummus using the main recipe (page 139), adding ½ cup (65 g) pineapple chunks, 3 mint leaves, and a dash of cayenne pepper (optional). Blend until smooth.

Garlic Tip: To roast garlic, preheat the oven to 400°F (200°C). Cut off the head of the garlic so that the tops of the cloves are exposed. Place the garlic in a piece of aluminum foil, drizzle with 1 teaspoon olive oil, wrap tightly, and bake for 40 minutes. Let cool, then squeeze each clove out of its skin.

MINI CRUSTLESS QUICHES

Prep Time 5 minutes
Cook Time 20–25 minutes
Yield 12 regular quiches or
36 mini quiches
Storage 4 days in fridge or
3 months in freezer

These mini quiches are full of protein and healthy vegetables. If your little one is having a chunky vegetable aversion, try pulsing the vegetables in the food processor for a couple of seconds until it turns into a thick tapenade before mixing in with the egg mixture.

 ## SPINACH, ROASTED RED BELL PEPPER, AND FETA MINI QUICHES *(shown opposite)*

This Mediterranean-inspired quiche is a family favorite—not only is it big on taste, but it is also full of iron-rich green leafy spinach.

Ingredients:
- 8 eggs
- ½ cup (15 g) packed spinach, finely chopped
- ½ cup (70 g) roasted red bell pepper, finely chopped
- ¼ cup (15 g) whole wheat breadcrumbs
- ½ teaspoon finely chopped fresh oregano
- ¼ cup (50 g) plain Greek yogurt
- ¼ cup (60 ml) unsweetened milk of choice
- salt and pepper, to taste
- ½ cup (60 g) feta, crumbled

1 Preheat the oven to 350°F (180°C) and spray or grease a regular 12-hole muffin pan or a 36-hole mini muffin pan with olive oil.
2 Whisk the eggs in a bowl and add the spinach, bell peppers, breadcrumbs, oregano, yogurt, milk, and some salt and pepper, and mix until just incorporated.
3 Fill the cups of the muffin pan two-thirds full and sprinkle with the feta. Do not overfill or the egg mixture will run over the sides of the pan. I like to sprinkle a little more black pepper on top, but that is optional.
4 Bake for 20–25 minutes or until the cheese is bubbly brown and the eggs are cooked. Let cool for 5 minutes and serve.

SPINACH, ROASTED RED BELL PEPPER, AND FETA MINI QUICHES, PAGE 142

variation | LEEK, ZUCCHINI, AND THYME MINI QUICHES

Make the quiches using the main recipe (page 142), omitting the spinach, red bell peppers, oregano, and feta and adding ½ cup (30 g) finely chopped leek, ½ cup (60 g) finely chopped zucchini, and 1 teaspoon chopped fresh thyme to the egg mixture. Fill the muffin pan with the quiche mixture and sprinkle with ½ cup (55 g) grated sharp white cheddar. Bake as instructed in the main recipe.

variation | TURKEY SAUSAGE, MUSHROOM, AND ARUGULA MINI QUICHES

Make the quiches using the main recipe (page 142), omitting the spinach, red bell peppers, oregano, and feta and adding ½ cup (75 g) cooked ground turkey sausage, ¼ cup (15 g) finely chopped mushrooms, and ½ cup (10 g) finely chopped arugula to the egg mixture. Fill the muffin pan with the quiche mixture and sprinkle with ½ cup (55 g) grated Gouda cheese. Bake as instructed in the main recipe.

variation | CARROT, PARSNIP, AND PARSLEY MINI QUICHES

Make the quiches using the main recipe (page 142), omitting the spinach, red bell peppers, oregano, and feta and adding ½ cup (70 g) shredded carrots, ½ cup (70 g) shredded parsnip, ¼ cup (10 g) finely chopped parsley, and ¼ teaspoon ground nutmeg to the egg mixture. Fill the muffin pan with the quiche mixture and sprinkle with ½ cup (55 g) grated cheddar cheese. Bake as instructed in the main recipe.

CLOSER LOOK
Pasture-Raised Products

When looking at purchasing meat or dairy products for your little ones, consider looking for brands that feature 100-percent grass-fed meat and products. Pasture-raised products are higher in omega-3 fatty acids and are available for beef, chicken, pork, lamb, milk, eggs, yogurt, butter, and cheese products. Pasture-raised animals are allowed to graze in a pasture all year round and eat healthy grasses and insects instead of processed foods. Rearing animals on a natural diet improves the quality of the food product and maximizes nutrients. If you cannot find these pasture-raised foods in the grocery store, consider looking around your local farmer's markets for a farm that provides these products.

SANDWICH STATIONS

Prep Time 5 minutes
Cook Time none
Yield 2 servings or
4 stick sandwiches
Storage 2 days in fridge

Want to see your toddler get excited about their food? There is a whole range of ways you can change up this simple lunch staple for a more exciting meal. Create a sandwich station, pop into pita pockets, or serve the sandwich ingredients on a stick for a fun twist.

 ## CAPRESE SANDWICH STATION WITH BASIL DIP

(shown on page 146)

An added bonus is that these recipes also include a fun dip. Perfect for dipping if serving on a stick or drizzling over your sandwich ingredients—now we are talking!

Ingredients:
- 8 cherry tomatoes
- 8 mini mozzarella balls
- 8 small cubes of French bread (or any loaf)
- 4 whole black olives, pitted

For the basil dip:
- 6 basil leaves
- 3 tablespoons olive oil
- 3 tablespoons balsamic vinegar
- 1 teaspoon honey
- ½ garlic clove
- salt and pepper

1 To make a sandwich station: Chop up all the ingredients in to pea-size pieces and serve on a platter.
To make a sandwich-on-a-stick: Thread a tomato, mozzarella ball, cube of bread, and olive onto a skewer and then repeat with bread, mozzarella ball, and tomato. Cut off the sharp end of the skewer and make sure no splinters are left.
2 To make the dip, put all the ingredients in a blender or food processor, and blend until everything is incorporated.
3 Serve the basil dip as a side for your stick sandwiches or sandwich station.

Skewer Tip: If you are serving older children their sandwiches on a stick, I have found that thicker wooden skewers (with the sharp end cut off) or lollipop sticks work great because you can cut them to the perfect length and they aren't sharp enough for your toddler to hurt themselves.

CAPRESE SANDWICH STATION WITH BASIL DIP, PAGE 145

variation | CHICKEN, BELL PEPPERS, AND CHEDDAR SANDWICH STATION WITH CILANTRO DIPPING SAUCE

Make a sandwich station or a sandwich-on-a-stick as instructed in the main recipe (page 145), using 8 cubes of cooked chicken, 8 thick-cut red bell pepper slices, and 8 squares of cheddar cheese. For the sandwich-on-a-stick, repeat twice on each skewer. Make dip as instructed in the main recipe, using ¼ cup (10 g) packed cilantro, ¼ cup (50 g) Greek yogurt, ½ garlic clove, 1 teaspoon honey, and a dash of cayenne pepper.

variation | ASIAN MEATBALL, PINEAPPLE, AND GREEN BELL PEPPER SANDWICH STATION WITH PEANUT DIPPING SAUCE

Make a sandwich station or sandwich-on-a-stick as instructed in the main recipe (page 145), using 4 Asian meatballs (Sesame Seed and Cilantro Meatballs, page 150, work great for this recipe) cut in half, 8 chunks of pineapple, and 8 thick-cut green bell pepper slices. For the sandwich-on-a-stick, repeat twice on each skewer. Make dip as instructed in the main recipe, using ¼ cup (60 ml) canned coconut milk, 2 tablespoons peanut (or almond) butter, 2 tablespoons rice vinegar, 1 tablespoon lime juice, and 1 tablespoon soy sauce.

variation | TURKEY, CUCUMBER, GOUDA, AND BLACKBERRY SANDWICH STATION

Make a sandwich station or sandwich-on-a-stick as instructed in the main recipe (page 145), using 8 cubes of cooked turkey, 8 half-cut cucumber slices, 8 squares of Gouda, and 4 blackberries. For the sandwich-on-a-stick, add the ingredients to each stick in the order listed above, then continue with Gouda, cucumber, and turkey. Make dip as instructed in the main recipe, using 3 tablespoons Greek yogurt, 3 tablespoons honey, 2 tablespoons yellow or grain mustard, and some pepper to taste.

MINI MEATBALLS

Prep Time 5 minutes
Cook Time 15 minutes
Yield 30–36 meatballs
Storage 4 days in fridge or
3 months in freezer

These little nuggets of goodness are great for first finger foods, a quick toddler lunch, or as a family dinner. Packed with protein-healthy meat, nutrient-dense vegetables, and spices, these recipes will give you plenty of ideas for quick meals to satisfy the whole family.

KALE AND PEAR MEATBALLS

You can serve these meatballs over your favorite pasta, inside a sandwich, or chopped and mixed into some mac and cheese. Meals planned for the rest of the month, check!

Ingredients:
- 1 lb (450 g) ground chicken
- ¼ cup (60 g) applesauce or apple puree
- ½ cup (30 g) pear, shredded and pressed (see Shredding Tip, page 106)
- ½ cup (30 g) kale, finely chopped
- ¼ cup (20 g) green onions, finely chopped
- 1 egg
- ½ cup (25 g) whole wheat breadcrumbs
- ½ teaspoon ground cumin
- salt and pepper, to taste

1 Put all the ingredients in a large bowl and gently fold everything together with your hands until well incorporated. Let the meat mixture sit while you preheat the oven to 450°F (230°C). Line a baking sheet with a silicon mat or aluminum foil that is sprayed with olive oil.

2 Roll the meat mixture into 1-inch (2.5-cm) balls—they can be smaller if you are making meatballs for baby finger food. I find it helps to wet your hands throughout the process.

3 Place the meatballs on the baking sheet and bake for 12–15 minutes or until the meatballs are cooked all the way through and gently brown. Let cool slightly and serve.

Also Good With: While I use different meats in each of the meatball recipes, you can use beef, pork, turkey, or chicken in any of the variations on page 150.

Use Your Meatballs: Other great ideas for using these versatile meatballs are: for the inside of a slider, as a topping for pizza night, mixed into your favorite soup, or even on top of your favorite salad.

CARROT, FETA, AND CHIVE MEATBALLS, PAGE 150

variation | SESAME SEED AND CILANTRO MEATBALLS

Make the meatballs as instructed in the main recipe (page 148), using 1 lb (450 g) ground beef, ⅓ cup (15 g) finely chopped cilantro, ⅓ cup (15 g) finely chopped spinach, ½ cup (25 g) whole wheat breadcrumbs, 1 egg, 2 tablespoons finely chopped green onion, 1 tablespoon sesame seeds, 1 teaspoon minced ginger, 1 minced garlic clove, and 1 tablespoon sesame oil. Sprinkle each meatball with some sesame seeds before baking.

variation | CARROT, FETA, AND CHIVE MEATBALLS

(shown on page 149)

Make the meatballs as instructed in the main recipe (page 148), using 1 lb (450 g) ground chicken, ½ cup (120 g) applesauce or apple puree, ½ cup (70 g) shredded carrots, ½ cup (60 g) feta, crumbled, 2 tablespoons finely chopped chives, 1 egg, ½ cup (25 g) whole wheat breadcrumbs, ½ teaspoon ground cumin, ¼ teaspoon ground nutmeg, and salt and pepper to taste.

variation | SUN-DRIED TOMATO AND BASIL MEATBALLS

Make the meatballs as instructed in the main recipe (page 148), using 1 lb (450 g) ground beef, ½ cup (50 g) parmesan, ½ cup (25 g) whole wheat breadcrumbs, ⅓ cup (35 g) chopped and drained sun-dried tomatoes in oil, ½ cup (15 g) finely chopped basil, 1 egg, ½ teaspoon dried oregano, 1 minced garlic clove, and some salt and pepper to taste.

Also Good With: At my house we absolutely love these meatballs served over pasta with a fresh pesto sauce.

variation | BEET AND SPINACH MEATBALLS

Make the meatballs as instructed in the main recipe (page 148), using 1 lb (450 g) ground turkey, ½ cup (120 g) applesauce or apple puree, ½ cup (70 g) shredded and pressed beets (any variety), ½ cup (15 g) finely chopped spinach, ¼ cup (20 g) finely chopped green onions, 1 egg, ½ cup (25 g) whole wheat breadcrumbs, ½ teaspoon ground cumin, ½ teaspoon garlic powder, and some salt and pepper to taste.

FRUIT LEATHER

Prep Time 5 minutes
Cook Time 3 hours
Yield 16 rolls of fruit leather
Storage 1 month

While three hours might seem like a long time to devote to making fruit leather, it really is an easy recipe—blend some fruit, honey, and spices; pour onto a baking sheet; and put into the oven. Since this fruit leather is full of fiber and vitamins, it is a perfect toddler snack.

 PLUM AND BASIL FRUIT LEATHER *(shown on pages 152–153)*

When you cut the leather up and take your first bite you will be in pure snack heaven! While it's totally acceptable to eat half the tray yourself, try to leave a couple of pieces for your toddler.

Ingredients:
- 3 cups (450 g) plums, pitted and chopped
- 2 tablespoons honey
- 4 basil leaves

1 Preheat the oven to 170°F (75°C). Line a baking sheet with a silicon mat. You can also use aluminium foil or parchment paper, but the leather will not be as flat.
2 Put all the ingredients in a blender or food processor, and blend for 1 minute or until smooth. Pour the fruit puree onto the baking sheet to about ⅛ inch (3 mm) thickness, and spread evenly with a spatula.
3 Bake for 3 hours, opening the oven door every hour or so to let some of the hot air escape. After three hours, check if the leather is done, the leather should be dry but still a little tacky. Depending on your oven, this may take another 1–2 hours. Remove from oven and let cool completely.
4 If using a silicon mat or aluminium foil, peel the leather away from the mat and place on a piece of parchment paper. Use a pizza cutter or scissors to cut into strips or bites. If using parchment paper, just roll it up with paper between the leather to stop the fruit leather from sticking together.

 variation | PEAR, APPLE, AND CINNAMON FRUIT LEATHER
(shown on pages 152–153)

Make as instructed in the main recipe (above), using 2 cups (450 g) cored, peeled, and chopped pears; 1 cup (150 g) cored, peeled, and chopped eating apples; 1 tablespoon lemon juice; and 1 teaspoon ground cinnamon.

variation | STRAWBERRY AND MINT FRUIT LEATHER

(shown below)

Make as instructed in the main recipe (page 151), using 3 cups (450 g) hulled strawberries, 3 tablespoons honey, and 6 mint leaves.

variation | PEACH AND ALMOND FRUIT LEATHER

Make as instructed in the main recipe (page 151), using 3 cups (450 g) pitted, peeled, and chopped peaches; 2 tablespoons honey; 1 tablespoon lemon juice; and 1 teaspoon almond extract.

PEAR, APPLE, AND CINNAMON FRUIT LEATHER, PAGE 151

Frozen Fruit: If you don't have the fresh fruit called for in these fruit leather recipes, simply use frozen fruit that has been thawed.

STRAWBERRY AND MINT FRUIT LEATHER, PAGE 152

PLUM AND BASIL FRUIT LEATHER, PAGE 151

CRISPY BROWN RICE TREATS

Prep Time none
Cook Time 10 minutes
Yield 20 treats
Storage 1 week in fridge

Full of natural sweetener, nut butter, and crispy gluten-free brown rice cereal, these treats also have additional protein, fiber, and heart-healthy fats. These yummy bites are where it's at!

 CRISPY BROWN RICE TREATS *(shown opposite)*
These are sure to be a hit in a school lunch, as an on-the-go snack, or as a treat to share at a potluck party.

Ingredients:
- 2 tablespoons coconut oil
- ¾ cup (180 ml) brown rice syrup
- ¾ cup (180 g) peanut or almond butter
- 6 cups (1.3 kg) brown rice cereal

1 Grease an 8 x 8 inch (20 x 20 cm) or 9 x 13 inch (23 x 32 cm) baking dish with coconut oil, then set aside.
2 Melt the coconut oil in a large saucepan over medium heat. Stir in the brown rice syrup and peanut butter and continue to stir until bubbles break the surface. Remove from heat. Add the brown rice cereal and mix until well combined.
3 Pour the rice crispy mixture into the prepared baking dish and firmly pat down until all areas of the pan are evenly covered and the mixture is sticking together.
4 Place in the fridge for 30 minutes and let set. Cut into squares and store in an airtight container in the fridge.

Brown Rice Syrup Tip: When choosing a brand of brown rice syrup, choose an organic option to limit the amount of contaminants. While brown rice syrup works well in this recipe, it is still a sweetener and should be consumed in moderation. If you want to try a different option, agave syrup also works well.

CRISPY BROWN RICE TREATS, PAGE 154

variation | CHOCOLATE AND HAZELNUT CRISPY BROWN RICE TREATS

Make as instructed in the main recipe (page 154), replacing the peanut butter with the Hazelnut and Chocolate Butter (see page 136) or any other organic chocolate spread. In addition, heat ½ cup (80 g) dark chocolate chips in a small saucepan, stirring constantly, then pour it over crispy brown rice treats in the baking dish before chilling until it is set.

variation | CRUNCHY ALMOND BUTTER CRISPY BROWN RICE TREATS *(shown opposite)*

Make as instructed in the main recipe (page 154), using almond butter and adding ½ cup (80 g) finely chopped salted almonds. In addition, heat ⅓ cup (80 g) almond butter in a small bowl until just warm, then drizzle over the crispy brown rice treats in the baking dish before chilling until it is set.

variation | TOASTED COCONUT AND MACADAMIA NUT CRISPY BROWN RICE TREATS

Make as instructed in the main recipe (page 154), adding ½ cup (35 g) toasted coconut and ½ cup (60 g) chopped macadamia nuts while mixing.

> **Sticky Hands Tip:** When pressing the crispy rice mixture into the pan, I have found that either greasing my hand or putting a plastic sandwich bag over my hand helps the mixture not to stick to my fingers as much.

CRUNCHY ALMOND BUTTER CRISPY BROWN RICE TREATS, PAGE 156

FRUITY ICE POPS

Prep Time 5 minutes
Freeze Time 4 hours
Yield roughly 2 cups (450 g) of puree will make six 3 oz (85 g) popsicles
Storage 3 months in freezer

When the summer heat is putting your kids on edge, these delicious popsicles are a tasty treat to cool them down. And since each pop is packed with vital nutrients, you won't mind when your kids start asking for them at breakfast!

 NECTARINE AND BASIL ICE POPS *(shown opposite and page 160)*
Using almost too ripe nectarines will make these pops extra sweet. If you can't find fresh nectarines, peaches are also great in this recipe.

Ingredients:
* 1 lb (450 g) ripe nectarines, pitted, peeled, and chopped
* 2 basil leaves, finely chopped
* ¼ cup (60 ml) water
* 4 tablespoons honey

1 Put all the ingredients in a blender or food processor and blend for 60 seconds or until the mixture is completely smooth.
2 Pour the nectarine mixture into popsicle molds, leaving a little space at the top for the mixture to expand. Insert popsicle sticks and place in the freezer for 4–5 hours.
3 To unstick the molds, run the molds under warm water for 10 seconds, then gently remove the ice pops.

 variation | STRAWBERRY, VANILLA, AND COCONUT CREAM ICE POPS
Make the ice pops as instructed in the main recipe (above), using 4 cups (600 g) hulled strawberries, 2 teaspoons vanilla extract, 2 tablespoons water, and 4 tablespoons honey, strain the mixture through a fine mesh colander if your kids don't like seeds. Gently fold in ¼ cup (60 ml) coconut cream or canned coconut milk until just swirled through before pouring into the popsicle molds and freezing.

 variation | ORANGE, GOLDEN BEET, CARROT, AND GINGER ICE POPS
Make the ice pops as instructed in the main recipe (above), adding 3 peeled and chopped oranges, 1 small peeled and chopped golden beet, 1 small peeled and chopped carrot, and 1 teaspoon freshly grated ginger to a high-speed blender or juicer. Add ¼ cup (60 ml) water and 4 tablespoons honey and stir. Pour into popsicle molds and freeze as instructed in the main recipe.

NECTARINE AND BASIL ICE POPS, PAGE 158

variation | COCONUT, PINEAPPLE, AND AVOCADO ICE POPS

Make the ice pops as instructed in the main recipe (page 158), using 1 ripe pitted and sliced avocado, 1 cup (130 g) fresh pineapple chunks, ½ cup (120 ml) canned coconut milk or cream, 1 tablespoon lemon juice, and 3 tablespoons honey. Only freeze for 1 hour to start with, without the popsicle sticks being added, then take the mold out and sprinkle ¼ cup (20 g) shredded coconut evenly onto molds. Press down gently so the coconut sticks, insert the popsicle sticks, and return the molds to the freezer for another 4 hours.

NECTARINE AND BASIL ICE POPS, PAGE 158

BANANA ICE CREAM

Prep Time 5 minutes
Freeze Time 14 hours
Yield 4 large servings
Storage 2 months in freezer

Whereas most ice creams are loaded with refined sugar and cream, this recipe is easy to make and only includes one main ingredient: bananas. Full of potassium and fiber, this ice cream is clean from all major allergens (nuts, gluten, dairy, and soy) and has no added sugar.

 ## SIMPLE BANANA ICE CREAM

The best part about this great recipe is that your little ones will never guess it is only made with bananas!

Ingredients:
- 4 ripe bananas, peeled and chopped into small, even pieces
- ½ teaspoon ground nutmeg

1 Place the banana pieces in an airtight container, a freezer bag, or on a lined baking sheet; place in the freezer and freeze overnight.
2 Transfer the frozen banana pieces to a blender or food processor, and pulse until they start to incorporate. Blend for 3–5 minutes, scraping down the sides as needed. Be patient; it will look like oatmeal at first, but after a couple of minutes the bananas will turn into thick and smooth ice cream.
3 Transfer to an airtight container and place in the freezer until frozen, roughly 1 hour. Spoon into dishes, sprinkle with nutmeg, and serve.

PEANUT BUTTER CRUNCH ICE CREAM, PAGE 162

variation | PEANUT BUTTER CRUNCH ICE CREAM

(shown opposite and on page 161)

Make the ice cream using the main recipe (page 161), omitting the nutmeg. Just as you are seeing the creamy smooth ice cream form in the food processor, add ⅓ cup (80 g) crunchy peanut butter and pulse for another 5 seconds. Continue as instructed in the main recipe, then right before serving, heat ¼ cup (60 g) chunky peanut butter in the microwave or stove top until just warm, and serve the ice cream drizzled with warm peanut butter.

variation | DOUBLE CHOCOLATE BANANA ICE CREAM

Make the ice cream as instructed in the main recipe (page 161), omitting the nutmeg. Just as you are seeing the creamy smooth ice cream form in the food processor, add 3 tablespoons cocoa powder and blend until well combined. Add 2 tablespoons dark chocolate pieces and pulse for 3–5 more times to break down the chocolate pieces. Continue as instructed in the main recipe.

variation | STRAWBERRY, BANANA, AND BASIL ICE CREAM

Make the ice cream as instructed in the main recipe (page 161), omitting the nutmeg and adding 1 cup (150 g) strawberries and 4 fresh basil leaves to the blender. Continue as instructed in the main recipe.

PEANUT BUTTER CRUNCH ICE CREAM, PAGE 162

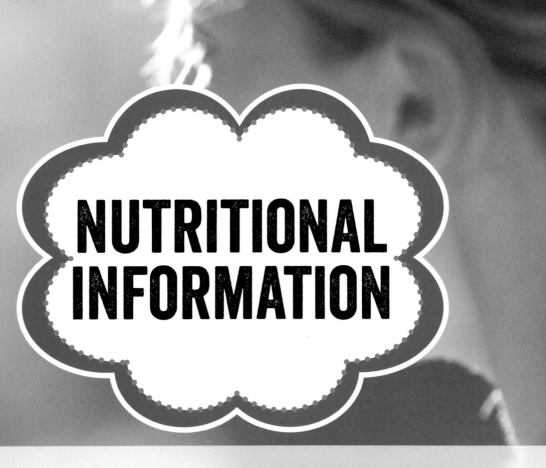

NUTRITIONAL INFORMATION

It is important to give your child the best possible start in life. During these early years essential growth and development take place. It is also a time when your little one is most receptive to new tastes and flavors, so starting them off with delicious purees packed full of nutritious whole foods and new flavors can help to establish a lifelong healthy relationship with food. Use this chapter to find out more about your baby's nutritional needs in their first years and to find the best recipes for your baby.

NOTES FOR THE RECIPES IN THIS BOOK

There are notes and tips throughout the book to guide you through the recipes and in preparing delicious whole foods for your baby. On this page you will find some key things to bear in mind when making yummy purees, snacks, and meals for your little ones.

Broth

Broth is a gut-healthy ingredient that can be added into purees for your baby and to toddler meals. Store-bought broths can be a hidden source of sodium, so make sure that you always choose no- or low-sodium broths when shopping or, even better, make your own broth to use in recipes.

Dairy and Non-Dairy Milks

Dairy products, including milk, are a great source of protein for your baby. Non-dairy alternatives, such as plant-based milks and yogurts, do not have the same protein content for your baby. If you are using plant-based milks, always choose the unsweetened varieties.

Honey for Babies

Honey is not suitable for children under one year of age. If a recipe calls for honey to serve to a younger baby, use maple syrup instead.

Nuts and Seeds

Nuts and seeds are nutritional powerhouses that are great to introduce to your baby's or toddler's diet. Nuts and seeds can be given in a pureed consistency. However, whole nuts and seeds are not suitable for children under the age of four, as they may be a choking hazard. If you are concerned about introducing nuts or seeds to your baby, speak with your pediatrician.

Cooking with Fish

Fish is a fantastic food to include in your baby's and toddler's diet, packed full of healthy fats and nutrients. When purchasing fish, always try to buy sustainable, organic produce. Make sure that any fish you cook with is skinned and that all the bones have been removed.

Organic Produce

Whenever possible, try to use organic produce when making food for your baby or toddler. Organic produce is full of nutritional goodness and has been grown without the use of any chemicals. (See panel on page 123 for more information.)

Combination Purees

Combination purees are a delicious next step for your baby after they've mastered simple first purees. Always introduce new foods to your baby as a simple puree first before starting any combination purees. This is especially important for any foods that may be allergens, such as fish.

Reheating Food

Making a big batch of food for your baby and freezing in portion sizes is my favorite way to make baby food. When reheating food for your baby, always make sure that you heat the food all the way through, then leave to cool before serving. It is especially important to check the internal temperature of food when using a microwave to reheat.

CHOOSING A RECIPE FOR YOUR BABY

Choosing how, what, and when to start feeding your baby can be a bit overwhelming. This book is packed full of delicious recipes to inspire you to start introducing nutrient-dense whole foods to your little one. Over the next few pages, you will find additional nutritional information to help you choose the best foods for your baby, as well as indexes of the recipes for a quick reference guide.

Finding the Right Recipe

Use the indexes and charts in this chapter to help you choose a delicious meal for your baby:

Top five recipes for essential nutrients (see pages 168–169)
Though most of the essential nutrients that your baby needs will still come from breastmilk or formula in the first stages of weaning, you can sneak in some extra nutrients to support their growth and development with the recipes in this book.

Index of recipes by key nutritional benefit (see pages 170–173)
Throughout this book, each recipe is tagged for key nutritional benefits to highlight both key nutrients, such as iron, protein, and carbohydrates, and some of the amazing health benefits that whole foods can provide.

General index (see pages 174–175)
There are useful tips and notes throughout the book, which may be helpful when you are cooking up that next batch of purees for your baby. If you have a particular question about preparation methods or ingredients, turn to pages 174–175 to find the information you need.

Nutritional Guidelines

There is a wealth of information and nutritional guidelines available on how to feed your baby and toddler. You can find this information from local government or organizations such as the American Academy of Pediatrics, the World Health Organization, and UNICEF. Always remember that nutritional information is designed as a rough guide to nutritional needs, and your baby's specific nutritional needs will be as unique as they are. Use nutritional information as a guide, but always watch out for your baby's signals and talk to your pediatrician.

Your baby will not be meeting their calorie requirements from food for some time and will continue to get most of their calorie and nutrient requirements from breastmilk or formula. Breastmilk is packed full of nutrients essential for healthy growth and development and is the best way to ensure a healthy start for your baby. If using formula, look out for those that contain added DHA. DHA has been identified as a vital nutrient in breastmilk that can have an important and positive impact on brain development.

Initially, the introduction of foods to your baby's diet is for experience and development. It is your opportunity to set your child up with a healthy relationship with food for life and to get those taste buds hooked on the delicious goodness of whole foods—and the delicious recipes in this book will do exactly that. It is always advised that you go to your pediatrician with any concerns you have about your baby's eating, feeding, development, or health.

TOP 5 RECIPES FOR ESSENTIAL NUTRIENTS

Whole foods are a fantastic way of providing all the essential nutrients needed for healthy growth and development. Highlighted below are my top five favorite recipes for the key nutrients that support healthy growth—iron and protein—and also essential functions supported by the nutrients in whole foods, so when your baby needs a little extra immunity boost or digestive help, you can quickly find the recipe you need.

Bone Growth

1 Sweet Potato and Curry Puree (page 44)
2 Beet and Mint Puree (page 56)
3 Roasted Banana Pancakes with Coconut Cream (page 112)
4 Pumpkin Spice and Pecan Granola (page 115)
5 Super Simple Hummus (page 139)

Iron Rich

1 Roasted Fall Vegetables with Chicken and Thyme Puree (page 58)
2 Beef and Oregano Puree (page 72)
3 Seared Tofu, Ginger, and Curry (page 90)
4 Toasted Coconut and Dark Chocolate Balls of Energy (page 134)
5 Asian Meatball, Pineapple, and Green Bell Pepper Sandwich Station with Peanut Dipping Sauce (page 147)

Protein Rich

1 Thai Chicken and Green Bean Puree (page 51)
2 Oat, Avocado, and Spinach Puree (page 68)
3 Salmon, Lime, and Parsley (page 89)
4 Roasted Almond and Vanilla Butter (page 135)
5 Turkey Sausage, Mushroom, and Arugula Mini Quiches (page 144)

Eases Digestion

1 Pear and Cinnamon Puree (page 34)
2 Peach, Plum, and Blueberry Puree (page 42)
3 Broccoli, Pear, Pea, and Mint Puree (page 49)
4 Sesame Seed and Cilantro Meatballs (page 150)
5 Plum and Basil Fruit Leather (page 151)

Immunity Builder

1 Spiced Carrot Puree with Coconut Milk (page 48)
2 Roasted Beets and Thyme (page 86)
3 Kiwi, Kale, and Mint Green Smoothie (page 99)
4 Kid-Friendly Orange Poppy Seed Muffins (page 107)
5 Pumpkin Pie Spice Fruit Dip (page 128)

INDEX OF RECIPES BY KEY NUTRITIONAL BENEFIT

Throughout the book, recipes are tagged for key nutritional benefits for your baby. Use the lists below as quick reference guides to match a recipe with your baby's specific nutritional needs, such as meals to provide a good source of protein to promote healthy growth or an immune-boosting puree to give your little one an extra boost ahead of cold and flu season.

Bright Eyes

High in Omega-3

Eases Digestion

GENERAL INDEX

Note: Page numbers in bold type indicate illustrations.

ACKNOWLEDGMENTS

Just as it takes a village to raise kids, it takes a village to write a book. As much as I would like to say it was all me, it actually took a ton of amazing people to put this book together.

First, I have to give a huge thank you to my parents for watching my little spitfires so I could work (and get the occasional pedicure) on this book. You have both encouraged me to find my passion and live that dream from day one, and you still continue to encourage that independence in me and now my girls.

Thank you Francie for playing with Parker on the days I needed to get out of the house and write.

Erica, Allison, Rachel, Lindsey, Jules, Breezy, Jen, Lauren, Kimmy, Jamie, and Mary: I am so glad I get to call you my friends and that I can always count on one of you to get a drink with me.

Hugs to Abi, my editor, for always being my cheerleader and not minding when I come back with crazy-sounding text with words that don't actually exist. Also, thank you to everyone at Quantum Publishing for putting together such an amazing book; it is absolutely beautiful!

Thank you Sara and Katie for all your nutrition smartness.

E and P, I love you both top to bottom, side to side, and all around, even when you don't like one of my new recipes.

Andy, you are still my rock. Thank you for believing in me and not giving me grief over how much I spend on coffee during the writing process.

My biggest thanks, as always, goes to my readers. I had no idea how amazing a community of health-minded mamas (and papas) could become. You inspire and push me more than you will ever know. Thank you to my early readers (you know who you are) for following and supporting me from the very beginning. I love seeing your amazing and healthy babies flood across my screen. If you are new to this community, don't hesitate to reach out and connect. I am always on Instagram and get back to readers daily @babyfoode. And you can always email me at hello@babyfoode.com; even though I am a little slower at responding, I do get back to each and every email I receive.

Publisher: Kerry Enzor
Editorial: Philippa Davis and Emma Harverson
Copyeditor: Abi Waters
Proofreader: Jane Bamforth
Nutritional Evaluators: Leslie L. Barton M.D. and Anne Marie Berggren
Designer: Tokiko Morishima
Photographer: Simon Pask
Production Manager: Zarni Win